GREEN
READS

Recent Titles in the
Children's and Young Adult Literature Reference Series
Catherine Barr, Series Editor

GREEN READS

Best Environmental
Resources for Youth, K–12

LINDSEY PATRICK WESSON

Children's and Young Adult Literature Reference
Catherine Barr, Series Editor

LIBRARIES UNLIMITED
An Imprint of ABC-CLIO, LLC

A B C   C L I O

Santa Barbara, California • Denver, Colorado • Oxford, England

Library of Congress Cataloging-in-Publication Data
Wesson, Lindsey Patrick.
  Green reads : best environmental resources for youth, k–12 / Lindsey Patrick Wesson.
    p. cm. — (Children's and young adult literature reference series)
  Includes bibliographical references and indexes.
  ISBN 978-1-59158-834-4 (hard copy : alk. paper) — ISBN 978-1-59158-835-1 (ebook) 1. Environmental education—Audio-visual aids. 2. Conservation of natural resources—Bibliography. 3. Conservation of natural resources—Juvenile literature—Bibliography. 4. Ecology—Bibliography. 5. Ecology—Juvenile literature—Bibliography. 6. Environmental protection—Bibliography. 7. Environmental protection—Juvenile literature—Bibliography. I. Title.
  GE75.W47 2009
  016.33372—dc22
                          2009017353

13 12 11 10 9   1 2 3 4 5

This book is also available on the World Wide Web as an eBook.
Visit www.abc-clio.com for details.

ABC-CLIO, LLC
130 Cremona Drive, P.O. Box 1911
Santa Barbara, California 93116-1911

This book is printed on acid-free paper ∞

Manufactured in the United States of America

DEDICATION

This book is for:

My mother, Jennifer. You are my tree: comforting me with your arms open wide and teaching me to grow.

My father, John. You are my soil: sometimes hard, sometimes soft, but willing to get your hands dirty in this most righteous fight.

My husband, Peter. You are my rock: supporting me through all kinds of weather and teaching me how to be strong.

My nieces and nephews, Ben, Liam, LeeLee, Gillian, Finn, and Elle, you are my sun: each shining brightly with hope and your awesome spirit for life.

ACKNOWLEDGMENTS

Special thanks to Catherine and Catharine for making this happen.

CONTENTS

PREFACE

I AM FORTUNATE TO BE A PRODUCT OF THE 1980S. Not because of the acid-washed jeans or spectacular bangs, but because the adults in my life were beginning to understand the importance of environmental conservation. In school, I learned about the greenhouse effect, the hole in the ozone layer, and how *not* to be a litterbug. We celebrated Earth Day by picking up the trash around the school and joining hands in a pledge to keep the Earth clean. I vividly remember one day in the third grade when a park ranger visited our class. She showed us a picture of a duck with a set of plastic loops (the type used to hold six-packs) around its neck. She asked us if we would want to wear someone else's garbage around our necks for the rest of our lives. I most certainly did not. We were taught to cut up these plastic loops before putting them in the trash. Whenever I see those loops, the image of that duck pops into my head. I have even been known to dig loops out of the trash to snip them.

I now know to avoid that kind of packaging altogether, but the fact remains that children's relationship to the environment is formed from an early age and is influenced by the education they receive and the behavior of the adults in their lives. I was also fortunate that my conscientious parents reinforced the environmental concepts I learned in school. That is why I wanted to write this book. The number of children's books published about the environment has steadily grown since my youth. It is my intention that this book be used as a resource for teachers, librarians, environmental educators, and parents to choose the best environmental books for the young people in their lives.

....

CRITERIA FOR INCLUSION

There are many wonderful fiction and nonfiction books available about our amazing world and the plants and animals that coexist with us. Books such as these help children and teens develop an awareness of and love for the environment. Once they have that awareness, young people can learn about the various threats to ecosystems. The books, CDs, and DVDs included in this book address those threats and the future of the environment.

Chapter 1 includes titles that explore why global warming is occurring; the effects that climate change is having on landscapes, habitats, and health; and what needs to be done to prevent global warming from escalating. Chapter 2 contains titles that look at the global problem of pollution, and how this in turn creates even larger problems such as global warming and habitat destruction. Chapter 3 focuses on titles that address the Earth's natural resources as well as energy resources such as solar, wind, geothermal, and nuclear power. While it is important to present the threats that the environment faces, it is even more important to provide solutions. Therefore Chapter 4 focuses on recycling and Chapter 5 on conservation, both recommending titles with information on the science, history, present, and future of these strategies.

It was important to me that the resources included in this book represent the most current information available. Therefore, the nonfiction titles were published during and since 2004. Fiction titles may date back to 1999. Some titles remain relevant longer than others, so the Recycled Favorites sections found in some chapters feature fiction titles published before 1999 and nonfiction titles published before 2004.

Viewpoints

The titles included in this book were chosen for their fair and accurate representation of environmental topics. I believe that global warming is a *human* problem greatly affected by *human* behavior, and most of the resources included in this book reflect that viewpoint. However, some of the titles represent what I consider "opposing viewpoints" devoting either part or the entire book to that alternate view. These titles can be found in the Subject Index under the heading "Opposing viewpoints" and the annotations note that the book presents many different perspectives.

Exclusions

Included in this book are resources that I recommend for environmental education. Titles that I felt were not useful, based on their organization or content, were not included. Although I made every possible effort to review as many of the available environmental titles that fit my criteria as I could, it is safe to assume that I missed some. Readers should not assume that exclusion from this book means that a resource is not valuable. Any excluded resources should be evaluated before deciding to use them or recommend them to children.

Two valuable types of books not included in this bibliography are general nature titles and books about endangered animals. It was important to me to include as many titles devoted to environmentalism as possible. Therefore, only resources that offer a generous amount of information about conservation, recycling, pollution, global warming, and energy resources were considered.

ORGANIZATION

The text is divided into five chapters, each listing entries under the headings Fiction and Nonfiction. Entries are arranged alphabetically by the author's last name, or by title when there is no author.

Each entry includes author (where applicable), title, illustrator (where applicable), series title, publisher, publication date, ISBN, number of pages, price, and grade level range (I personally find age ranges incredibly subjective, so have made these ranges broad; I always recommend basing your selections on the level of the prospective reader). Subject headings give the user a quick summary of the content; the Subject/Grade Level Index allows the user to identify other books with these subjects. The bibliographic material is followed by an annotation intended to present a basic summary of the item, some of its features, and the best use for the book, DVD, or CD. Finally, there are three symbols, which are explained later in the Preface.

Here are examples of standalone titles, series titles with a single author, and series titles with multiple authors.

Standalone Title

4   Lewis, Anne Margaret. *Santa Goes Green.*
GRADES: PS–2
Ill. by Elisa Chavarri. Mackinac Island Press, 2008, ISBN 978-1-934133-16-3, 32p. $15.95.
SUBJECTS: Christmas—Fiction; Polar bears—Fiction; Global warming—Fiction

Finn is concerned about his polar bear friend, Leopold, and writes to ask Santa for help. Together, Finn and Santa visit Leopold to find out about the effects of global warming and Santa agrees to help spread the word. This lively and adventurous tale is energized by delightfully expressive and comic illustrations. A perfect story to read at the beginning of the holiday season. 🌳

Series Titles with Single Author

Desonie, Dana.
SERIES: OUR FRAGILE PLANET. Chelsea House

18   *Climate: Causes and Effects of Climate Change.*
GRADES: 6–12
2007, ISBN 978-0-8160-6214-0, 194p. $35.00.
SUBJECTS: Climate change; Global warming

19   *Polar Regions: Human Impacts.*
GRADES: 6–12
2008, ISBN 978-0-8160-6218-8, 194p. $35.00.
SUBJECTS: Ecology—Polar regions; Polar regions; Nature—Effects of human beings on

The books in this series are structured very much like middle school textbooks in both appearance and content. These two entries deliver information about the effects of global warming on the Earth's climate and its arctic regions in a manner that is appropriate for this age group. Photographs, charts, and diagrams combine with vocabulary words, a glossary, and an index to complete these useful books. ♻ 🌍

Series Titles with Multiple Authors

SERIES: SCIENCE MATTERS. Weigl Publishers

134 Hudak, Heather C. *Air Pollution.*
GRADES: 2–4
2007, ISBN 978-1-59036-415-4, 24p. $24.45.
SUBJECTS: Air pollution

135 Ostopowich, Melanie. *Water Pollution.*
GRADES: 2–4
2006, ISBN 978-1-59036-307-2, 24p. $24.45.
SUBJECTS: Water pollution

The Science Matters series provides an introductory look into current science topics. The design draws the reader in and the clear text makes the books easy to read. These titles engage the reader with questions, experiments, and environmental tips. The quick pace and interesting subjects make this series a good choice for struggling and reluctant readers interested in science. ✿ ✪

Following the main text are two appendixes—Access by Symbol and Access by Series—and three indexes: Author, Title, and Subject/Grade Level.

Recycled Favorites

The Recycled Favorites sections that appear in most chapters include older titles that I still deem relevant and important. Nonfiction titles in these sections were published or produced before 2004, and fiction titles before 1999.

Watching and Listening Green

DVDs and CDs are listed in sections called Watching and Listening Green. Multimedia items relating to the environment are often more difficult to come by, but help to create a robust collection. In each case, the format is shown at the beginning of the bibliographic information.

Subchapters

Special subchapters on Green Science Fiction/Fantasy for Teens, Green People, Green Things, and Earth Day feature titles specific to those subchapters that do not necessarily fit into one of the other chapters.

Storytimes and Activities

At the end of each chapter, I have included a sample storytime using the titles found in the preceding pages. As a children's librarian, I felt it important to show just how easy it is to incorporate environmental books into your child's life. If I can create five storytimes devoted solely to environmental themes, think how easy it would be to work just one book into a lesson plan, story hour, or nighttime routine.

Also included in most chapters are activities for older children. These activities include ideas for class projects and field trips that reinforce the concepts discussed in the chapters.

Key to Symbols

The following symbols serve to quickly identify the nature of each title. Each entry has at least one symbol attached to it, and many have more than one.

- ♛ (Tree symbol) Indicates that the title has a lively or heart-filled tone. When this symbol is used alone, it generally means that the book is more entertaining than educational. When looking for books to read aloud or to use for a storytime, look for this symbol.
- ☻ (Earth symbol) Indicates that the title contains a generous amount of factual information. Look for this symbol to help a child or teen with an assignment or research question.
- ♺ (Recycle symbol) Indicates that the title contains practical and useful environmental tips for children and teens. Use this symbol to help children who are interested in getting involved in conservation efforts.

Note: The titles that have all three symbols are what I like to call the "Triple Solutions" (instead of the "Triple Threats"). These books are fun, educational, and environmentally useful. You can't ask for more than that in an environmental book for children and teens!

GLOBAL
WARMING

G LOBAL WARMING IS SCARY. NO MATTER HOW YOU look at it, the effects of global warming and climate change are frighteningly consequential. Some activists think this fear is a good thing because it forces action. However, developmentally, children and teens are dealing with so many changes, that they do not need more fear in their lives. Rather, they need to be informed on a level that they can comprehend and encouraged to draw their own conclusions based on the information they receive.

In the case of global warming, young children need just a basic introduction to the scientific concepts of the greenhouse effect and climate change in order to understand the consequences. Then, when provided with easy and useful everyday tips on how to make a difference, children can understand the impact that their actions have on the world. Older children are able to process more detailed scientific information and, depending on the child, may even enjoy the science. As children get older, their social awareness broadens, and while global implications may not appear as important as those close to home, they come to comprehend the connectedness of the world. For example, children are not always able to understand how the melting ice caps may affect their neighborhoods; but they will understand how this problem has affected the habitats and livelihoods of polar bears.

Teens' social awareness is much more pronounced. Not only can most teens comprehend the science of global warming, they are also in a better position to grasp the global implications. Teens need information that equips them with a strong understanding of the issues and long-term solutions and they should be aware of climate change studies and environmental policies.

The books in this chapter do not use fear to inform younger people about global warming. They use science, folktales, biographical information, research, useful tips, and sometimes even humor to tell the story of global warming. While it certainly can be scary, global warming can also be fascinating and children will be motivated by the hope that their actions can make a difference.

....

FICTION

1   Aston, Dianna Hutts. *Loony Little: An Environmental Tale.*
GRADES: PS–2
Ill. by Kelly Murphy. Candlewick Press, 2007, pap., ISBN 978-0-7636-3562-6, 40p. $6.99.
SUBJECTS: Global warming—Fiction; Animals—Fiction; Polar regions—Fiction

In this "Chicken Little" retelling, Loony Little sets off to tell the Polar Bear Queen that the polar ice cap is melting. Along the way, she meets some Arctic friends to help her on her quest. Murphy's bright pastel illustrations follow the group on its journey. Though the Polar Bear Queen does not seem too concerned about global warming, this book will help start a conversation with little ones. Also included, at the back of the book, is factual information about the Arctic animals featured in the book and about the effects of global warming on the polar region. 🌐 🌳

....

2   Bergen, Laura. *The Polar Bears' Home.*
GRADES: PS–2
SERIES: LITTLE GREEN BOOKS. Ill. by Vincent Nguyen. Little Simon, 2008, pap., ISBN 978-1-4169-6787-3, 24p. $3.99.
SUBJECTS: Polar bears—Fiction; Global warming—Fiction

This gentle book from Simon & Schuster's Little Green series follows a little girl and her father as they learn how global warming is affecting the lives of two baby polar bears. This book helps illustrate the impact that our actions have on the world and is balanced with tip on how kids can prevent global warming from escalating. This book would be a good choice for read-aloud and lapsit storytimes. ❀ 🌳

....

3   Fromental, Jean-Luc. *365 Penguins.*
GRADES: PS–2
Ill. by Joelle Jolivet. Abrams Books, 2006, ISBN 978-0-8109-4460-2,
48p. $17.95.
SUBJECTS: Penguins—Fiction; Mathematics—Fiction; Global
warming—Fiction

A family receives an interesting package on New Year's Day, and for the ensuing year another penguin arrives at the house each day. It turns out that Uncle Victor has been sending the penguins because global warming has made their natural habitat difficult. This is a funny story that covers many math concepts as the family struggles to cope with the new arrivals. It also features some geography and big descriptive illustrations, making it a hit for the classroom. 🍄

....

4   Lewis, Anne Margaret. *Santa Goes Green.*
GRADES: PS–2
Ill. by Elisa Chavarri. Mackinac Island Press, 2008, ISBN 978-1-934133-16-3, 32p. $15.95.
SUBJECTS: Christmas—Fiction; Polar bears—Fiction; Global
warming—Fiction

Finn is concerned about his polar bear friend, Leopold, and writes to ask Santa for help. Together, Finn and Santa visit Leopold to find out about the effects of global warming and Santa agrees to help spread the word. This lively and adventurous tale is energized by delightfully expressive and comic illustrations. A perfect story to read at the beginning of the holiday season. 🍄

....

5   Okimoto, Jean Davies. *Winston of Churchill: One Bear's Battle Against Global Warming.*
GRADES: PS–2
Ill. by Jeremiah Trammell. Sasquatch Books, 2007, ISBN 978-1-57061-543-6, 32p. $16.95.
SUBJECTS: Polar bears—Fiction; Global warming—Fiction

This is the inspiring tale of a group of polar bears who decide to take action against global warming the only way they know how. At the helm of this polar bear protest is a bear named Winston who rallies the others together and even stops smoking his famous cigar. A delightful tale with expressive and colorful illustrations, this book is sure to be a crowd-pleaser and makes a fun read-aloud for kindergarten and first-grade audiences. ♺ 🌳

....

6   Perla, Victoria. *When Santa Turned Green.*
GRADES: PS–2
Ill. by Mirna Kantarevic. Thomas Nelson, 2008, ISBN 978-1-4003-1384-6, 48p. $15.99.
SUBJECTS: Global warming—Fiction; Environmental protection—Fiction; Christmas—Fiction

We know that global warming affects polar bears, but what about other Arctic residents? When Santa begins to realize that the North Pole is melting because of global warming, he decides it's time to spring into action. Enlisting the help of all the children who receive presents, Santa learns about what causes global warming and what steps can be taken to alleviate the effects of climate change. Full of helpful tips and unique, colorful, and expressive illustrations, this clever story is an entertaining addition to Christmas and environmental collections. ♺ 🌳

....

7   Tara, Stephanie Lisa. *Snowy White World to Save.*
GRADES: PS–2
Ill. by Alex Walton. Brown Books, 2007, ISBN 978-1-933285-89-4, 32p. $16.95.
SUBJECTS: Polar bears—Fiction; Global warming—Fiction

Told in simple, beautiful verse, this picture book is an excellent choice for very young readers. By following a day in the life of a polar bear and her cubs, children see how the melting ice has affected them. Slightly melancholy, the lulling verse and emotive illustrations send a strong message that even the youngest ears will hear. This book is highly recommended for toddler or preschool storytime and for lapsit reading or bedtime; it includes a resource guide for more information. 🌳

WATCHING AND LISTENING GREEN

8   *Global Warming: Public Agenda and Government Responsibility.*
GRADES: 9–12
DVD. Disney Educational, 2007, ISBN 978-1-59753-161-0,
$49.95.
SUBJECTS: Global warming

Appropriate for high school science and civics students, this DVD provides a broad look at the various issues surrounding global warming.
Rather than handling the topic as a debate, this program contends that
global warming is real, that it is caused by greenhouse gases, and that
those greenhouse gases are a result of human behavior. The eight short
clips are segments from ABC News programs on topics including the effects of global warming on Arctic regions and the political aspects of environmental policies. Also included are discussion questions and an
interactive DVD-ROM that educators can use to supplement their lessons. ☻

9   Gold, Daniel B., and Judith Helfand, dirs. *Everything's Cool.*
GRADES: 10–12
DVD. Bullfrog Films, 2007, ISBN 978-0-9793607-2-5, $295.00.
90 minutes
SUBJECTS: Global warming; Climate change

Produced by Bullfrog Films, this investigative documentary for high
school students examines the gap between scientific opinion and popular opinion of the dangers of global warming. This 90-minute film features interviews with journalists, scientists, and activists who believe
the threat of global warming is real and evident. It then looks at opposing viewpoints and examines the sources of funding and support for
scientists who refute global warming. An intriguing look at the effect
that politics and the media have on the information that the public receives about the environment. ☻

10   Gore, Al, and Davis Guggenheim, dir. *An Inconvenient Truth:
A Global Warning.*
GRADES: 9–12

DVD. Paramount, 2006, ISBN 978-1-4157-2478-1, $29.98. 96 minutes

SUBJECTS: Global warming; Greenhouse effect; Environmental policy

The award-winning documentary by former Vice President Al Gore offers a pointed look at the very real crisis of global warming. The film is an adaptation of a slide show developed to explain the scientific evidence supporting climate change and the role that humans have played in it. Interspersed with news footage and interviews with Gore, this documentary is appropriate for middle and high school audiences (although best discussed in smaller segments). It's hard to talk about the environment without this documentary being brought up, so it will help students to be familiar with it. ♺ 🌏

11   Odegard, Unni. *On Thin Ice.*
GRADES: 7–10
DVD. Landmark Media, 2007, $195. 25 minutes
SUBJECTS: Global warming; Climate change; Polar regions; Svalbard

A scientist travels to northern Svalbard to see the changing environment caused by the melting ice and how it is affecting seals and other Arctic life. Dramatic and sad, this program emphasizes the dangers that global warming has created for this habitat and its ice-dependent animals. Viewers see a newborn seal, then a diagram that illustrates the alarming rate at which the seal's habitat is disappearing. This 25-minute video is an emotional and educational resource that truly captures a serious issue. Highly recommended for middle and high school audiences. 🌏

12   Petersen, Jan Tandrup, and Rikke Lauridsen. *Global Warming in the Arctic: The Melting of Svalbard.*
GRADES: 9–12
DVD. Landmark Media, 2007, $195. 28 minutes
SUBJECTS: Global warming; Svalbard; Polar regions

Viewers follow a scientist as he explores Svalbard, on the edge of civilization in the Arctic, and observes the effects of global warming on this area that is home to polar bears, walruses, and Arctic foxes. Svalbard has experienced dramatic melting and many species are struggling to survive in this changing environment. Best suited for high school audiences, this video dramatically captures the environment that is being most affected by the changing climate. ◐

---

13 **Ravetch, Adam, and Sarah Robertson, dirs.** *Arctic Tale.*
GRADES: K—5
DVD. Paramount Home Entertainment, 2007, ISBN 978-1-4157-3547-3, $29.99. 86 minutes; Writing Credits: Linda Woolverton, Mose Richards, and Kristen Gore
SUBJECTS: Global warming; Polar bears; Walrus; Polar regions

This documentary follows the lives of a walrus family and a polar bear family and looks at how each survives in the Arctic. What is especially clear is that the changing climate has made survival more challenging for all Arctic life. This documentary is told in a manner that younger children will understand and there is not any exceedingly disturbing material. However, this is a realistic program that could be difficult for sensitive audiences. An excellent way to illustrate the impact of global warming on Arctic animals. ◐ ♛

---

14 **Wilson, Steve, et al.** *The Eyes of Nye: Global Climate Change.*
GRADES: 7—10
DVD. Disney Educational, 2005, ISBN 978-1-59753-027-9, $49.95. 23 minutes
SUBJECTS: Global warming; Climatology

Science Guy Bill Nye helps students understand global warming. By exploring how scientists measure climate change, how carbon dioxide affects the atmosphere, and how humans rely on fossil fuels, this video covers a lot of difficult information yet is accessible to middle and high school audiences thanks to humorous clips, animated explanations, and interviews. An educator's guide provides additional material. ♻ ◐ ♛

....

NONFICTION

15   Barr, Gary. *Climate Change: Is the World in Danger?*
GRADES: 5–8
SERIES: BEHIND THE NEWS. Heinemann, 2007, ISBN 978-1-4034-8830-5, 56p. $32.86.
SUBJECTS: Climate change

Articles about climate change that have been selected from prominent newspapers around the world are analyzed in this entry in the Behind the News series. Students can examine what's behind the information found in a typical newspaper article. A valuable resource for students who need to debate or defend topics concerning climate change. ☻

....

16   Berne, Emma Carlson. *Global Warming and Climate Change.*
GRADES: 9–12
SERIES: COMPACT RESEARCH. ReferencePoint Press, 2008, ISBN 978-1-60152-019-7, 112p. $25.95.
SUBJECTS: Global warming; Climate change

Report writers will appreciate this book in the Compact Research series and its broad look at the subjects of global warming and climate change. Primary sources, diagrams, illustrations, statistics, and subject overviews help the reader comprehend the material. The books in this series also include information about key people and organizations concerned with environmental studies. ☻

....

17   Bily, Cynthia A., ed. *Global Warming.*
GRADES: 9–12
SERIES: OPPOSING VIEWPOINTS. Greenhaven Press, 2006, ISBN 978-0-7377-2935-1, 208p. $37.40.
SUBJECTS: Global warming; Climate change; Opposing viewpoints

Part of a respected series, this is a truly balanced perspective on global warming. Well-edited articles examine different opinions about the causes of and problems created by climate change, allowing readers to develop critical-thinking and research skills. Complementing the articles are occasional diagrams, charts, and cartoons. Annotated bibliographies, comprehension questions, and fact boxes make this a one-stop resource on global warming for older readers. ☽

....

18 Bishop, Amanda. *Climate Change.*
GRADES: 2–4
SERIES: SAVING OUR WORLD. Marshall Cavendish, 2008, ISBN 978-0-7614-3219-7, 32p. $28.50.
SUBJECTS: Climate change; Global warming

Large photographs and brief paragraphs combine to examine global warming's adverse effects on the Earth's landscape. The scientific and social impacts of climate change are explained, with helpful tips and comprehension questions rounding out the book. ♻ ☽

....

19 Biskup, Agniesezka. *Understanding Global Warming with Max Axiom, Super Scientist.*
GRADES: 3–5
SERIES: GRAPHIC SCIENCE. Ill. by Cynthia Martin and Bill Anderson. Capstone Press, 2008, ISBN 978-1-4296-0139-9, 32p. $28.45.
SUBJECTS: Global warming

Max Axiom takes the reader on a scientific journey exploring the causes and effects of global warming. While the subject may be less exciting than the plots of most graphic novels, the format may draw in reluctant students. Short facts, a glossary, and bibliographies add to the book's value as a research resource. ☽ ♟

....

20 Burnie, David. *Endangered Planet.*
GRADES: 4–8
SERIES: KINGFISHER KNOWLEDGE. Kingfisher, 2007, pap., ISBN 978-0-7534-6160-0, 64p. $8.95.
SUBJECTS: Nature—Effect of human beings on; Pollution; Environmental responsibility

Bright photographs and bold headings draw attention to the Earth's changing environment. This book explores the delicate and often destructive relationship between humans and nature. Fact-filled paragraphs are enlivened with charts, diagrams, and dramatic side-by-side photographs that illustrate how the Earth has been affected by global warming and population growth. Chapter summaries, a glossary, and "Go Further" bibliographic boxes add to the value of this book. ●

21   Cheel, Dr. Richard. *Global Warming Alert.*
GRADES: 3–6
SERIES: DISASTER ALERT! Crabtree Publishing, 2007, ISBN 978-0-7787-1587-0, 32p. $19.95.
SUBJECTS: Global warming

Most of the books in this series deal with acute disasters; this volume explores the causes and effects of the long-term problem of global warming. The short chapters—combined with bright graphics, diagrams, and photographs—add to the appeal. Also helpful are tips on how to help slow global warming, a glossary, and an index. ●

22   Cherry, Lynne, and Gary Braasch. *How We Know What We Know About Our Changing Climate: Scientists and Kids Explore Global Warming.*
GRADES: 4–8
SERIES: SHARING NATURE WITH CHILDREN. Dawn Publications, 2008, ISBN 978-1-58469-103-7, 66p. $17.95.
SUBJECTS: Climate change; Global warming

While keeping the outlook positive, this book makes the issue of climate change accessible and real. The first section, "Where We Find Clues About Climate Change," encourages readers to actively examine the effects of climate change through examples and experiments. The other three sections provide applicable science and activism ideas to help readers take action and work together to fight global warming. The vivid pictures, extensive bibliography, and resource list make this book a remarkable resource for middle school readers. A teacher's guide is also available. ♻ ● ♛

23   David, Laurie, and Cambria Gordon. *The Down-to-Earth Guide to Global Warming.*
GRADES: 4–7
Scholastic, 2007, ISBN 978-0-439-02494-5, 112p. $15.99.
SUBJECTS: Global warming

A must-have for any environmental collection. Bold text, bright photographs, colorful diagrams, and even cartoon illustrations keep the reader's attention, and the content holds up its end of the bargain, too, with chapters such as "It's Getting Hot in Here" and "Extinction Stinks." The authors provide plenty of scientific and age-appropriate information about global warming and what children can do to help. ⚙ ❂ ♣

---

24   Dean, James M. *Bodies from the Ice: Melting Glaciers and the Recovery of the Past.*
GRADES: 4–6
Houghton Mifflin, 2008, ISBN 978-0-618-80045-2, 64p. $17.00.
SUBJECTS: Global warming; Glaciers; Ice mummies

When mountain climbers came across a frozen human body in the melting ice of the Niederjoch Glacier, they knew the body was ancient. Radiocarbon dating revealed it to be 5,300 years old, from the Copper Age! This fascinating book examines this incredible find and other discoveries from the past that are being revealed as glaciers continue to melt. The historical and scientific information is interesting and complete, and the pictures (and their inherent gross-out factor) will draw readers in. ❂

Desonie, Dana.
SERIES: OUR FRAGILE PLANET. Chelsea House

25   *Climate: Causes and Effects of Climate Change.*
GRADES: 6–12
2007, ISBN 978-0-8160-6214-0, 194p. $35.00.
SUBJECTS: Climate change; Global warming

26   *Polar Regions: Human Impacts.*
GRADES: 6–12
2008, ISBN 978-0-8160-6218-8, 194p. $35.00.
SUBJECTS: Ecology—Polar regions; Polar regions; Nature—Effect of human beings on

The books in this series are structured very much like middle school textbooks in both appearance and content. These two entries deliver information about the effects of global warming on the Earth's climate and its arctic regions in a manner that is appropriate for this age group. Photographs, charts, and diagrams combine with vocabulary words, a glossary, and an index to complete these useful books. ⚙ ❂

27   Farrar, Amy. *Global Warming.*
GRADES: 7–10
SERIES: ESSENTIAL VIEWPOINTS. Abdo Publishing, 2007, ISBN 978-1-
59928-859-8, 112p. $32.79.
SUBJECTS: Global warming

The Essential Viewpoints series examines current issues and presents a balanced look at the factors behind them. This book includes a generous amount of statistical, biographical, and legislative information about global warming issues. Also useful are the timelines, Web sites, bibliographies, and glossaries. Text boxes include information such as notable global warming scientists and anecdotes about the topic. Organizational contact information and other resources help readers explore global warming further. ♻ 🌐

28   Foxxe, Ellen. *Rising Seas: Shorelines Under Threat.*
GRADES: 7–12
SERIES: EXTREME ENVIRONMENTAL THREATS. Rosen Publishing, 2007,
ISBN 978-1-4042-0742-4, 64p. $29.25.
SUBJECTS: Sea level; Coast changes; Climate change

Climate change is causing sea levels to rise, affecting marine life and coastal areas. This book, part of the Extreme Environmental Threats series, helps make this aspect of climate change more real to students. While geared toward students in grades 7–12, the layout and length will appeal to younger audiences or to older students with lower reading skills. Tables, fast facts, color photographs, an extensive bibliography, a glossary, and an index make this a valuable research tool. 🌐

29   Freedman, Jeri. *Climate Change: Human Effects on the Nitrogen Cycle.*
GRADES: 7–12
SERIES: EXTREME ENVIRONMENTAL THREATS. Rosen Publishing, 2007,
ISBN 978-1-4042-0744-8, 64p. $29.25.
SUBJECTS: Climate change; Nitrogen cycle; Global warming; Nature—
Effect of human beings on

With intriguing chapter titles such as "The End of Life As We Know It?" and "The Future Is in Our Hands," this book deftly captures readers' interest. It first explains how humans are affecting the changing climate and then explores how the changing climate is affecting the environment. Part of the

Extreme Environmental Threats series, this volume also describes ways in which humans can follow a more sustainable course. The sensationalist tone will appeal to young adults and the high-quality content will appeal to educators. 🌐

---

30   **Fretwell, Holly Lippke.** *The Sky's Not Falling: Why It's OK to Chill About Global Warming.*

GRADES: 4—6

World Ahead Publishing, 2007, pap., ISBN 978-0-9767269-4-4, 128p. $17.95.

SUBJECTS: Global warming; Environmental policy; Opposing viewpoints

This is the only title in this bibliography that is dedicated solely to the "opposing viewpoint." Fretwell posits that global warming is part of a cyclical phenomenon and is not affected by human behavior. It is important to recognize titles such as this because students need to be aware that there are other viewpoints to consider. This book has been included to represent a view that may be the preferred perspective of some readers.

---

31   **Friend, Robyn C., and Judith Love Cohen.** *A Clean Sky: The Global Warming Story.*

GRADES: 2—4

Ill. by David A. Katz. Cascade Pass, 2007, ISBN 978-1-880599-82-2, 48p. $13.95.

SUBJECTS: Global warming; Climate change

This book details the science behind global warming and climate change in an understandable and unintimidating way. The conversational tone and frequent analogies deftly explain the challenges facing the planet and strategies to protect it. Complementing the text are colorful illustrations, fun facts, a list of environmental careers, and an in-depth glossary. ♻ 🌐

---

32   **Gore, Al.** *An Inconvenient Truth: The Crisis of Global Warming.*

GRADES: 6—9

Viking Children's, 2007, ISBN 978-0-670-06271-3, 192p. $25.00.

SUBJECTS: Global warming; Climate change; Environmental protection

A companion to the award-winning documentary of the same name, this book brings the same urgent message to a younger audience. Using many of the vivid and startling images from the documentary to illustrate the effects of climate change, the text appeals to younger audiences without speaking down to them or sacrificing timeliness. The content is accessible, the graphics are bold and evocative, and the binding and pages are made of high-quality material. These features make this book a necessary addition to any science collection. ⊛ ❂

---

33   Green, Robert. *Global Warming.*

GRADES: 4–8

SERIES: GLOBAL PERSPECTIVES. Cherry Lake Publishing, 2008, ISBN 978-1-60279-123-7, 32p. $18.95.

SUBJECTS: Global warming

This book is ideal for readers who are reluctant to pick up nonfiction. The subject of global warming is anecdotally introduced through a conversation among students from many different countries. The students ask questions that prompt each chapter. The scientific information is accurate and relevant but accessible to even the most hesitant readers. ❂

---

34   Hall, Julie. *A Hot Planet Needs Cool Kids: Understanding Climate Change and What You Can Do About It.*

GRADES: 3–6

Ill. by Sarah Lane. Green Goat Books, 2007, pap., ISBN 978-0-615-15585-2, 88p. $15.99.

SUBJECTS: Global warming; Climate change

This book does an excellent job of explaining the greenhouse effect, climate change, and how scientists study global warming. Deftly balancing people's responsibility for global warming with helpful and useful ways in which people—specifically children—can fight global warming, this book is equal parts education and inspiration. The pages are energized with color photographs, dynamic illustrations, and occasional mini-biographies of eco-heroes. Factoring in the glossary, index, and bibliography, this book is a must-have resource for global warming education. ⊛ ❂ ♟

35   Haugen, David M., and Susan Musser, ed. *Is Global Warming a Threat?*
GRADES: 9–12
SERIES: AT ISSUE. Greenhaven Press, 2007, ISBN 978-0-7377-3687-8, 102p. $29.95.
SUBJECTS: Global warming; Opposing viewpoints

This series tackles current issues that are of interest to high school readers. In this entry, the editors have put together a collection of well-balanced essays that explore many sides of the issue, including "Global Warming Will Have Noticeable Impact" and "Global Warming Is Media-Hyped Hysteria." There are no photographs or diagrams, but the essays, bibliography, and organizational contacts deliver useful information. This is a valuable resource to help readers develop critical thinking skills. 🌐

SERIES: SCIENTIFIC AMERICAN CRITICAL ANTHOLOGIES ON ENVIRONMENT AND CLIMATE. Rosen Publishing

36   Human, Katy, ed. *Critical Perspectives on World Climate.*
GRADES: 9–12
2006, ISBN 978-1-4042-0688-5, 184p. $31.95.
SUBJECTS: Climate change

37   Viegas, Jennifer, ed. *Critical Perspectives on Planet Earth.*
GRADES: 9–12
2006, ISBN 978-1-4042-0687-8, 278p. $31.95.
SUBJECTS: Climate change

38   West, Krista, ed. *Critical Perspectives on the Oceans.*
GRADES: 9–12
2006, ISBN 978-1-4042-0692-2, 200p. $31.95.
SUBJECTS: Marine ecology

The books in this series consist of collections of *Scientific American* articles originally published between 1995 and 2005 that relate to the environment and climate. Most of the articles include black-and-white graphics such as diagrams, charts, and illustrations to complement the text. High school students will find these useful for reports about climate change, the Earth, and rising oceans. 🌐

39   Jakab, Cheryl. *Climate Change.*
GRADES: 3—6
SERIES: GLOBAL ISSUES. Smart Apple Media, 2008, ISBN 978-1-59920-123-8, 32p. $27.10.
SUBJECTS: Climate change

The problem of climate change is introduced to young readers in a highly accessible way. Examples of the global reach of this problem are followed by possible solutions. This helps students understand causes and effects of climate change while giving them a better understanding of and perspective on the impact of their everyday actions. The dynamic design adds interest to this valuable resource. 🌐

40   Johnson, Rebecca L. *Investigating Climate Change: Scientists' Search for Answers in a Warming World.*
GRADES: 6—9
SERIES: DISCOVERY! Twenty-First Century Books, 2008, ISBN 978-0-8225-6792-9, 111p. $31.93.
SUBJECTS: Climate change; Global warming

Readers will find comprehensive explanations of the greenhouse effect, carbon dioxide, altered ecosystems, weather changes, and rising seas, among other topics dealing with global warming. The book integrates side-by-side photographs, charts, and diagrams to show the effects of global warming and offers insights into the future. Includes environmental tips, an extensive glossary and bibliography, and a detailed index. ♻ 🌐

41   Johnson, Rebecca L. *Understanding Global Warming.*
GRADES: 3—5
SERIES: SAVING OUR LIVING EARTH. Lerner Publishing, 2009, ISBN 978-0-8225-7561-0, 71p. $30.60.
SUBJECTS: Global warming

"It's a fact: the earth is warming up," says this entry in the Saving Our Living Earth series. Readers will be inspired by the photographs of real children and young adults working to improve the environment. The detailed text, rich layouts, bold photographs, bibliography, index, and glossary are nice features that appear in all the books in this series. ♻ 🌐

ACTIVITIES FOR OLDER ENVIRONMENTALISTS

�֎ Hands-On Experiment ✶

Using two large glass jars placed in the sunlight, you can re-create global warming in your classroom. This experiment is described in *Planet Earth: 25 Environmental Projects You Can Build Yourself* and *Eco-Fun: Great Projects, Experiments, and Games for a Greener Earth*. After learning about global warming and the greenhouse effect from the books included in this chapter, conduct this experiment to track the rising temperatures created by trapped greenhouse gases. Ask your students to write down the changes in temperature of each jar at specific intervals throughout the day. Consider leaving the jars overnight to see how the temperature in each jar is changed by night temperatures. For younger children, create two large graphs shaped like thermometers, and allow students to color in the thermometers that correspond to the jars as their temperature heats up. For older students, use the temperature numbers to create math problems, such as the difference between the two, or the rate of acceleration.

42 Knight, M. J. *Why Should I Walk More Often?*
GRADES: 2—4
SERIES: ONE SMALL STEP. Smart Apple Media, 2009, ISBN 978-1-59920-268-6, 32p. $27.10.
SUBJECTS: Automobiles—Environmental aspects

After reading this book, children will understand that their actions affect the environment and that simple steps can help make a global difference. The two-page spreads include short, easy-to-read paragraphs, color photographs, and illustrations. "I Can Make a Difference" boxes and "One Small Fact" bubbles provide quick scientific or statistical information. A current and useful resource for young readers that includes a glossary, Web resources, and an index. ♺ 🌍

43 Kowalski, Kathiann M. *Global Warming.*
GRADES: 4—8
SERIES: OPEN FOR DEBATE. Benchmark Books, 2004, ISBN 978-0-7614-1582-4, 142p. $42.79.

SUBJECTS: Global warming; Opposing viewpoints

This series presents different sides of controversial issues. In the case of global warming, the evidence points to its reality and consequences. However, the author does explore arguments that global warming is not as severe or dire as some researchers report. An index and a bibliography help make this a solid recommendation for well-rounded research. 🌐

---

44   Lim, Cheng Puay. *Our Warming Planet.*
GRADES: 2–4
SERIES: GREEN ALERT! Raintree Publishers, 2004, ISBN 978-0-7398-7014-3, 48p.
SUBJECTS: Global warming

Bright photographs and brief chapters help keep readers interested in the causes and effects of global warming. Each chapter explores a different aspect of the subject for a rich introduction to this global concern. Other tools include case studies, environmental tips, a glossary, an index, and a bibliography. ♻ 🌐

---

45   Lishak, Antony. *Global Warming.*
GRADES: 3–5
SERIES: WHAT'S THAT GOT TO DO WITH ME? Smart Apple Media, 2008, ISBN 978-1-59920-037-8, 32p. $27.10.
SUBJECTS: Global warming

Through accounts of ten individuals, this book presents differing views on global warming and how people respond to it. Each chapter challenges the reader to ask questions and to participate through thought and action. Accompanying each chapter are quick facts and statistics relating to the person discussing global warming. The useful index, glossary, and bibliography also add to the value of this book, which is an excellent resource for teachers and students. 🌐

---

46   Lourie, Peter. *Arctic Thaw: The People of the Whale in a Changing Climate.*
GRADES: 5–8
Boyds Mills Press, 2007, ISBN 978-1-59078-436-5, 48p. $17.95.
SUBJECTS: Whaling—Environmental aspects; Climate change; Inupiat; Alaska

An interesting and intimate look at the native Inupiat of northern Alaska and how global warming has affected their way of life. Whaling provides the Inupiats' main livelihood and the melting ice has made this dangerous. Lourie tackles a serious and difficult subject and produces an interesting scientific journey partnered with an emotional narrative. Photographs enliven the text and complement the Inupiat story. ✪

....

47   Martins, John. *Ultraviolet Danger: Holes in the Ozone Layer.*
GRADES: 7–12
SERIES: EXTREME ENVIRONMENTAL THREATS. Rosen Publishing, 2007, ISBN 978-1-4042-0743-1, 64p. $29.25.
SUBJECTS: Ozone layer depletion; Climate change

The ozone layer is the focus of this book in the Extreme Environmental Threats series. Large text, fast facts, and color photographs help to engage the reader's interest and to explain how the ozone layer was discovered and what is causing its depletion. The bibliography, glossary, and index help to make this book a recommended resource for middle and high school collections. ✪

....

48   Miller, Debra A., ed. *Global Warming.*
GRADES: 7–12
SERIES: CURRENT CONTROVERSIES. Greenhaven Press, 2008, pap., ISBN 978-0-7377-4071-4, 189p. $25.95.
SUBJECTS: Global warming

The Current Controversies series uses brief, age-appropriate, and varied articles in comprehensive examinations of controversial subjects. In this book in the series, articles address the political tug-of-war over the issue and the potential causes and consequences of climate change. A list of organizations, a bibliography, and an index are included. ✪

....

49   Minkel, Dan, ed. *Global Warming.*
GRADES: 7–10
SERIES: INTRODUCING ISSUES WITH OPPOSING VIEWPOINTS. Greenhaven Press, 2006, ISBN 978-0-7377-3564-2, 112p. $33.70.
SUBJECTS: Global warming; Opposing viewpoints

Presenting brief, well-edited articles and examining both sides of the global warming debate, this book helps readers develop critical-thinking and research skills without using overly complicated language. This series serves a younger audience than the Opposing Viewpoints series but includes many of the trusted features of the series for older readers, including color photographs, occasional cartoons, an annotated bibliography, comprehension questions, and quick fact boxes. ☻

---

50   Morris, Neil. *Global Warming.*
GRADES: 5–7
SERIES: WHAT IF WE DO NOTHING? World Almanac Library, 2007, ISBN 978-0-8368-7755-7, 48p. $31.00.
SUBJECTS: Global warming

Readers are drawn into the subject of global warming through a hypothetical look at what could happen if nothing is done about our warming planet. Plainly written text, fast facts, charts, tables, photographs, a glossary, and an index all help readers to explore the causes and effects of global warming. Theoretical questions prompt the reader to consider possible solutions to this environmental problem. ♲ ☻

---

51   Nardo, Don. *Climate Crisis: The Science of Global Warming.*
GRADES: 5–7
SERIES: HEADLINE SCIENCE. Compass Point Books, 2009, ISBN 978-0-7565-3571-1, 48p. $20.99.
SUBJECTS: Global warming; Climate change

Each chapter in this book about climate change begins with a recent quote from a recognizable news source such as CBS and the *New York Times*. The book uses contemporary layouts, dramatic photographs, historical fact boxes, and a timeline to relay information about the consequences of global warming, the natural feedback process that is exacerbated by climate change, and government and individual initiatives to combat global warming. Includes bibliographic resources, a glossary, and source notes. ☻

---

52   Nardo, Don. *Ozone.*
GRADES: 3–6
SERIES: OUR ENVIRONMENT. Kidhaven Press, 2006, ISBN 978-0-7377-2630-5, 48p. $26.20.

SUBJECTS: Ozone; Greenhouse effect; Air pollution

How ozone is formed, what effects humans have on the ozone layer and the problems created by ozone loss are all explained in this entry in the Our Environment series. Colorful diagrams, photographs, and accessible vocabulary complete this high-quality resource focusing solely on the ozone layer. An important addition to a climate change collection. 🌐

Nelson, John.
SERIES: JR. GRAPHIC ENVIRONMENTAL DANGERS. PowerKids Press

53 *Global Warming: Greenhouse Gases and the Ozone Layer.*
GRADES: 3–6
2009, ISBN 978-1-4042-4260-9, 24p. $23.95.
SUBJECTS: Polar ice caps; Greenhouse effect

54 *Polar Ice Caps in Danger: Expedition to Antarctica.*
GRADES: 3–6
2009, ISBN 978-1-4042-4227-2, 24p. $23.95.
SUBJECTS: Polar ice caps; Greenhouse effect

The Jr. Graphic Environmental Dangers series uses a graphic novel format to address environmental issues. Featuring exciting stories based on fact, these entries convey the urgency of the problem of global warming and the melting polar ice caps. Equal parts entertainment and education, these books are good for reluctant readers and for children who need a nudge to get them started on their research. 🌐 🌳

---

55 **Parker, Russ.** *Climate Crisis.*
GRADES: 3–6
SERIES: PLANET IN CRISIS. Rosen Publishing, 2009, ISBN 978-1-4358-5254-9, 32p. $25.25.
SUBJECTS: Climate change; Greenhouse effect; Global warming

Contemporary layouts that are busy and bright invite readers to explore the subject of climate change by addressing the ozone layer and how the climate is affected by the greenhouse effect. Like the other books in the Planet in Crisis series, this book is large in size and features two-page spreads, "hot topic" boxes, progression charts, and diagrams. Includes organizational contacts, a bibliography, an index, and a glossary. ♻ 🌐

Parker, Russ.
SERIES: PLANET IN CRISIS. Rosen Publishing

56 *Pollution Crisis.*
GRADES: 3—6
2009, ISBN 978-1-4358-5252-5, 32p. $25.25.
SUBJECTS: Pollution

57 *Waste Management Crisis.*
GRADES: 3—6
2009, ISBN 978-1-4358-5253-2, 32p. $25.25.
SUBJECTS: Refuse and refuse disposal; Waste minimization

What effect does pollution have on habitats? What happens when we waste
the Earth's resources? Using bright layouts, contemporary photographs, "hot
topic" boxes, charts, and diagrams, these books in the Planet in Crisis series
also address the issue of dumping waste and why it is important to reduce
waste. They each include organizational contacts, a bibliography, an index,
and a glossary. ♺ 🌐

58 Parks, Peggy J. *Global Warming.*
GRADES: 3—6
SERIES: OUR ENVIRONMENT. Kidhaven Press, 2004, ISBN 978-0-7377-
1822-5, 48p. $26.20.
SUBJECTS: Global warming; Climate change

Parks examines the causes of global warming, the problems it creates, and
possible solutions to these problems. The issues—including the greenhouse
effect and climate change—are thoroughly examined using colorful diagrams, photographs, and well-placed definitions. Other helpful features in
this book are notes, a multimedia bibliography, a glossary, and indexes. 🌐

59 Revkin, Andrew C. *The North Pole Was Here: Puzzles and Perils at
the Top of the World.*
GRADES: 6—9
Kingfisher, 2006, ISBN 978-0-7534-5993-5, 128p. $15.95.
SUBJECTS: Polar regions; Polar regions; Global warming

A true account of a journalist who accompanied scientists to the North Pole
as they studied the effects of climate change on the landscape, this is a great
recommendation for fans of adventure stories. Scientific and historical in-

formation is deftly woven into the narrative and complemented by colorful graphics and illustrations. Adults will appreciate the educational aspect of this book, and children will love its adventure and mystery. ✪ ♟

---

60 Robinson, Matthew. *America Debates Global Warming: Crisis or Myth.*

GRADES: 5–8

SERIES: AMERICA DEBATES. Rosen Publishing, 2008, ISBN 978-1-4042-1925-0, 64p. $29.25.

SUBJECTS: Global warming; Opposing viewpoints

The America Debates series provides balanced examinations of all sides of issues of national concern. This volume uses short chapters, pictures, and fact boxes to present viewpoints from both sides of the environmental debate. Perfect for students working on debates or persuasive essays, this source also features an index, a glossary, a timeline, and a bibliography. ✪

---

61 Rockwell, Anne. *Why Are the Ice Caps Melting? The Dangers of Global Warming.*

GRADES: K–3

SERIES: LET'S-READ-AND-FIND-OUT SCIENCE 2. Ill. by Paul Meisel. Collins, 2006, ISBN 978-0-06-054669-4, 40p. $15.99.

SUBJECTS: Global warming; Greenhouse effect; Opposing viewpoints

Rockwell's global warming warning is cleverly disguised as a picture book with expressive and lively illustrations of people and places around the world. The gentle yet serious text explains global warming and even considers opposing viewpoints. The author packs a great deal of information into each page, including tips for young readers who may be concerned about global warming. ✪

---

62 Royston, Angela. *Global Warming.*

GRADES: K–2

SERIES: PROTECT OUR PLANET. Heinemann, 2008, ISBN 978-1-4329-0924-6, 32p. $25.36.

SUBJECTS: Global warming

Royston examines global warming—what's causing it and what can be done about it. Using photographs, timely facts and figures, charts, and diagrams, this book thoroughly explores the effects of global warming. "What Do You

Think?" and "What Can You Do?" boxes in each chapter aid comprehension and give readers tips on how they can relieve some of the planet's pressure. ⬡ 🌐

....

63   Simpson, Kathleen. *Extreme Weather: Science Tackles Global Warming and Climate Change.*
GRADES: 3–6
SERIES: NATIONAL GEOGRAPHIC INVESTIGATES. National Geographic, 2008, ISBN 978-1-4263-0281-7, 64p. $27.90.
SUBJECTS: Global warming; Climate change; Weather

How is "extreme" weather linked to global warming? Readers will find out that scientists use past weather patterns and present conditions to predict future weather. Diagrams and photographs enliven the accessible text. This book provides scientific proof that global warming is causing climate change. 🌐

....

64   Somers, Michael. *Antarctic Melting: The Disappearing Antarctic Ice Cap.*
GRADES: 7–12
SERIES: EXTREME ENVIRONMENTAL THREATS. Rosen Publishing, 2007, ISBN 978-1-4042-0741-7, 64p. $29.25.
SUBJECTS: Ice caps; Global warming; Polar regions

The impact of global warming on Arctic regions is the focus of this entry in the Extreme Environmental Threats series. While geared toward readers in grades 7–12, this will also appeal to younger audiences or to older students with lower reading skills. Students will find out that ice can predict future climate change. A bibliography, a glossary, and an index help to make this book a recommended resource for middle and high school collections. 🌐

....

65   Spilsbury, Louise. *Changing Climate: Living with the Weather.*
GRADES: 3–6
SERIES: GEOGRAPHY FOCUS. Raintree Publishers, 2006, ISBN 978-1-4109-1112-4, 48p. $31.43.
SUBJECTS: Climate change

Will we have to learn to live with more extreme weather as the earth's climate changes? In this volume in the Geography Focus series, photographs, diagrams, and charts keep the reader's attention while exploring this possibility. Each two-page spread uses short, information-packed paragraphs and "fast fact" boxes to convey ideas succinctly. Vocabulary words, a glossary, a bibliography, and an index add to the value of this book. ♻

---

66   Stille, Darlene R. *The Greenhouse Effect: Warming the Earth.*
GRADES: 5–7
SERIES: EXPLORING SCIENCE. Compass Point Books, 2007, ISBN 978-0-7565-1956-8, 48p. $20.95.
SUBJECTS: Greenhouse effect; Climate; Atmosphere

The emphasis of this book is more on content than design. Though it includes fact boxes and other elements that break up the text, it has a more sophisticated tone than do many books for this age group. Subtle fonts and graphics explain the relationship between the greenhouse effect and global warming, and the author's deep knowledge of the subject is evident. ♻

---

67   Stoyles, Pennie, and Peter Pentland. *Global Warming.*
GRADES: 2–4
SERIES: SCIENCE ISSUES. Smart Apple Media, 2004, ISBN 978-1-58340-328-0, 32p.
SUBJECTS: Global warming

A great resource for students researching an environmental hot topic, this book in the Science Issues series examines the different arguments for what causes global warming and what can be done about it. Comprehension questions are sprinkled throughout the book and a summary, a glossary, and an index are included. ♻

---

68   Tanaka, Shelley. *Climate Change.*
GRADES: 9–12
SERIES: GROUNDWORK GUIDES. Groundwood Books, 2007, pap., ISBN 978-0-88899-784-5, 144p. $9.95.
SUBJECTS: Global warming; Climate change

Part of the Groundwork Guides series, this book for young adults provides an overview of climate change without pulling any punches. Clear and succinct scientific evidence helps students come to a better understanding of a confusing and sometimes scary topic. Perhaps the most compelling feature of this book is the examination of why some people are unwilling to accept the fact that human activity is the cause of global warming. This book is a truly excellent resource for any young adult collection. ♻ ♻

....

69   Thornhill, Jan. *This Is My Planet: The Kids' Guide to Global Warming.*

GRADES: 3—6

Maple Tree Press, 2007, ISBN 978-1-897349-06-9, 64p. $21.95.

SUBJECTS: Global warming

From the bright red cover and empowering title to the colorful, dynamic layouts, this book entices young readers to explore the issues surrounding global warming. Each two-page spread is packed with color photographs, fact-filled boxes, vocabulary words, statistical information, and diagrams. The broad chapters are simply titled, and the "People" chapter contains hands-on information for readers interested in doing their part to help limit global warming. ♲ ◐ ♣

....

70   Unwin, Mike. *Climate Change.*

GRADES: 6—8

SERIES: PLANET UNDER PRESSURE. Heinemann, 2007, ISBN 978-1-4034-8216-7, 48p. $22.00.

SUBJECTS: Climate change; Global warming; Nature—Effect of human beings on

Photographs, timely facts and figures, charts, and diagrams help to answer readers' questions about climate change. Readers will be challenged to think for themselves by the "What Do You Think?" and "What Can You Do?" features in this book. ♲ ◐

....

71   Williams, Mary E., ed. *Writing the Critical Essay: Global Warming.*

GRADES: 7—12

SERIES: AN OPPOSING VIEWPOINTS GUIDE. Greenhaven Press, 2006, ISBN 978-0-7377-3210-8, 96p. $29.95.

SUBJECTS: Global warming; Opposing viewpoints

This book uses the characteristic Opposing Viewpoints strategies to help students think and write critically about global warming. The first section presents brief, well-written articles representing contrasting opinions on the issues of global warming and climate change. Writing examples and tools prompt thoughtful evaluation and research on the topic. ◐

GREEN SCIENCE FICTION/FANTASY FOR TEENS

The following titles are part of a growing number of environmental science fiction and fantasy books. These books are great recommendations for teen environmentalists and can produce interesting "what if . . . " discussions.

72 **Cooper, Susan.** *Green Boy.*
GRADES: 9—12
Margaret K. McElderry, 2002, ISBN 978-0-689-84751-6, 195p. $16.00.
SUBJECTS: Environmental protection—Fiction; Bahamas—Fiction
🌳

73 **Dean, Claire.** *Girlwood.*
GRADES: 9—12
Ill. by Aya Kato. Houghton Mifflin, 2008, ISBN 978-0-618-88390-5, 246p. $16.00.
SUBJECTS: Conservation of natural resources—Fiction; Nature—Fiction 🌳

74 **D'Lacy, Chris.** *The Fire Eternal.*
GRADES: 3—6
SERIES: THE DRAGON SERIES. Orchard, 2008, ISBN 978-0-545-05163-7, 512p. $16.99.
SUBJECTS: Dragons—Fiction; Supernatural—Fiction; Climate change —Fiction; Environmental degradation—Fiction 🌳

75 **D'Lacy, Chris.** *The Fire Star.*
GRADES: 3—6
SERIES: THE DRAGON SERIES. Orchard, 2008, ISBN 978-0-439-90185-7, 560p. $16.99.
SUBJECTS: Dragons—Fiction; Supernatural—Fiction; Climate change —Fiction; Environmental degradation—Fiction 🌳

76 **Griffin, Adele.** *Vampire Island.*
GRADES: 3—6
Putnam Juvenile, 2007, ISBN 978-0-399-23785-0, 128p. $14.99.
SUBJECTS: Environmental protection—Fiction; Vampires—Fiction
🌳

77   McNaughton, Janet. *The Secret Under My Skin.*
GRADES: 7–10
Eos, 2005, ISBN 978-0-06-008989-4, 272p. $15.99.
SUBJECTS: Science fiction—Fiction; Environmental
degradation—Fiction 🌳

78   Melling, O. R. *The Light-Bearer's Daughter.*
GRADES: 5–7
SERIES: THE CHRONICLES OF FAERIE. Amulet, 2007, ISBN 978-0-
8109-0781-2, 304p. $16.95.
SUBJECTS: Fairies—Fiction 🌳

79   Miyazaki, Hayao. *Nausicaa of the Valley of the Wind:*
Volume One.
GRADES: 7–12
SERIES: NAUSICAA OF THE VALLEY OF THE WIND. Ill. by the author.
VIZ, LLC, 2004, pap., ISBN 978-1-59116-408-1, 150p. $9.95.
SUBJECTS: Pollution—Fiction; Princesses—Fiction; Graphic
novels—Fiction 🌳

80   Nelson, Blake. *They Came From Below.*
GRADES: 9–12
Tom Doherty Associates, 2007, ISBN 978-0-7653-1423-9, 299p.
$17.95.
SUBJECTS: Marine pollution—Fiction; Radioactive pollution—
Fiction; Environmental protection—Fiction; Imaginary
creatures—Fiction 🌳

81   Thomas, Rob. *Green Thumb.*
GRADES: 6–8
Simon & Schuster, 1999, ISBN 978-0-689-81780-9, 192p.
SUBJECTS: Rain forests—Fiction; Environmental protection—
Fiction 🌳

GLOBAL WARMING STORYTIME

Begin with "Good Morning, Dear Earth."

Good morning, dear Earth
Good morning, dear Sun (hold your hands above your head)
Good morning, dear stones (put a "stone" in your hand)
And the flowers, every one. (make your hand into a flower)

Good morning, dear bees (fly a "bee" around between your fingers)
And the birds in the trees (make your arms into wings and flap them)
Good morning to you (point to the children)
And good morning to me. (point to yourself)

"Good morning, children. This morning we are going to read stories and sing songs about our Earth and the weather."

Hold up a picture or puppet of a polar bear.

"What is this animal? Do you know where this animal lives? Polar bears live in the Arctic. Is it hot where polar bears live or is it cold? We're going to read a story about a polar bear named Winston."

Read *Winston of Churchill: One Bear's Battle Against Global Warming* by Jean Davies Okimoto (see entry 5).

If you have a puppet (any arctic animal will do), you can have a conversation with the puppet about the book.

You: *"I didn't know that the ice caps were melting! What can I do to help?"*
Puppet: *"Every little bit helps. Walk or ride your bike instead of riding in the car. Turn off the lights and other electrical appliances when you aren't using them. If you need to drive somewhere, take the bus."*
You: *"I know a song about a bus! Let's sing 'The Wheels on the Bus' together!"*

Sing "The Wheels on the Bus."

"Well, if polar bears are affected by the ice caps melting, I wonder what other animals are affected? Let's read Loony Little *to find out!"*

Read *Loony Little: An Environmental Tale* by Dianna Hutts Aston (see entry 1).

Bring out the puppet again.

> You: *"I know I can help fight global warming. Tell me again what we should do."*
>
> Puppet: *"Walk when you can, instead of driving. Remember to turn off the lights and TV when you don't need them. And if you have to drive, take the bus!"*
>
> You: *"Hmm, I think a song might help us remember. Will everyone stand up and sing it with me?"*

Sing "Help Save the Earth" (to the tune of "Here We Go 'Round the Mulberry Bush").

> *This is the way we walk to the store (walk in place)*
> *Walk to the store, walk to the store*
> *This is the way we walk to the store*
> *To help save the Earth.*
>
> *Second verse: This is the way we turn off the lights (put your arms in the air and bring them down to cover your eyes)*
> *Third verse: This is the way we take the bus (sit down and stand up)*

"I hope we all remember to walk, ride our bikes, or take the bus when we can, and turn off the lights and TV when we aren't using them. If we all do that we can help fight global warming and save the ice caps. I know I will!"

Sing "If You Love Earth and You Know It" (to the tune of "If You're Happy and You Know It").

> *If you love Earth and you know it, clap your hands!*
> *If you love Earth and you know it, clap your hands!*
> *If you love Earth and you know it, then let your actions show it!*
> *If you love Earth and you know it, clap your hands!*
>
> *Second verse: If you love Earth and you know it, stomp your feet!*
>
> *Third verse: If you love Earth and you know it, shout "Reduce!"*
> *If you love Earth and you know it, shout "Reuse!"*
> *If you love Earth and you know it, then let your actions show it!*
> *If you love Earth and you know it, shout "Recycle!"*

POLLUTION

POLLUTION IS DIRTY. THIS IS AN UNDENIABLE FACT, AND helpful in terms of educating children and teens about pollution. While global warming can be somewhat abstract, pollution is tangible and it is easy to identify its causes and effects. Even the youngest child is able to recognize litter and understand that it belongs in the trash can or recycling bin. Small children may not be able to comprehend the science behind smog, but they can connect the exhaust from cars with the hazy cloud that is evident in big cities.

Because young children can identify the problems caused by pollution, it is often—and appropriately—the first environmental problem they learn about. Picture books and beginning readers offer descriptive illustrations, color photographs, and endearing stories and anecdotes that show the harmful impact of pollution.

After these books establish the problems relating to pollution, they use images and stories of young children to provide good examples of environmentally conscious behavior that will shape children's relationship with the Earth from an early age.

As readers mature, they are able to see the effects of pollution beyond their own communities. They understand scientifically how pollution changes habitats and how smog affects the health of plant and animal life. Older readers may be moved by the effects of pollution and be inspired to get involved in environmental activism. Many of the books geared toward older readers provide helpful tips for activism and information on environmental organizations.

The resources for both children and teens included in this chapter explain that humans produce waste (too much of it!) and that waste needs a place to go. Sometimes it ends up in landfills, to which there are limitations, and sometimes the waste ends up in the wrong places and affects the Earth's resources. Titles in this chapter encourage people to produce less waste and to dispose of it appropriately. Children are taught from very young ages to identify and solve problems. Pollution is an easy (albeit dirty) problem that is simple to identify and relatively uncomplicated to solve.

....

FICTION

82   Anholt, Laurence. *Eco-Wolf and the Three Pigs.*
GRADES: 2–4
SERIES: SERIOUSLY SILLY STORIES. Ill. by Arthur Robins. Compass Point Books, 2004, ISBN 978-0-7565-0630-8, 64p. $11.95.
SUBJECTS: Environmental protection—Fiction; Forest animals—Fiction; Pollution—Fiction

In this modern retelling of the "Three Little Pigs," Anholt reverses the roles and presents an environmentally conscious Eco-Wolf as the hero of this tale. Eco-Wolf must work together with his forest friends to prevent the polluting Pigs from destroying their land with urban sprawl. Anholt presents a cute tale with a somewhat stereotypical main character; Robins's black-and-white cartoon illustrations bring the silly characters to life. 🌳

....

83   Atwell, Debby. *River.*
GRADES: PS–2
Houghton Mifflin, 1999, ISBN 978-0-395-93546-0, 31p. $16.00.
SUBJECTS: Water pollution—Fiction; Rivers—Fiction

Vibrantly painted, full-page illustrations combine with simple text to describe the evolution of a river. In the beginning, the river is used as a natural resource for the people of the land. However, as more and more people use and abuse the river, its beauty and usefulness fade until it is unrecognizable. When the people realize the damage that the river has endured, they work together to restore it to its natural wonder. 🌳

....

84   Base, Graeme. *Uno's Garden.*
GRADES: PS–2
Ill. by the author. Harry N. Abrams, 2006, ISBN 978-0-8109-5473-1, 40p. $19.95.

SUBJECTS: Nature—Fiction; Pollution—Fiction; Overpopulation—Fiction

Uno discovers a beautiful, thriving garden with amazing plants and creatures, including one snortlepig. Time passes and more and more people discover Uno's garden. As it becomes more populated with people, it becomes less populated with plants and animals until finally the snortlepig is the only animal remaining. This beautifully illustrated story goes on to show how Uno passes on his respect for nature to his children and grandchildren and they work together to rebuild Uno's garden. This book received the 2007 Newton Marasco Foundation Green Earth Book Award for Children. 🌳

85   **Brimner, Larry Dane.** *Trash Trouble.*

GRADES: PS—2

SERIES: THE CORNER KIDS. Ill. by Christine Tripp. Children's Press, 2003, ISBN 978-0-516-22547-0, 32p. $20.50.

SUBJECTS: Refuse and refuse disposal—Fiction; Refuse and refuse disposal—Fiction; Environmental protection—Fiction

The Corner Kids learn about environmental responsibility in this Rookie Choices beginning reader. On a trip to the Nature Center, the children see firsthand how trash affects the environment and decide to do their part to prevent it from harming animals again. The simple text and story are supported by cartoon illustrations featuring a cast of multicultural children and adults. 🌳

86   **Drummond, Allan.** *Tin Lizzie.*

GRADES: PS—2

Ill. by the author. Farrar, Straus and Giroux, 2008, ISBN 978-0-374-32000-3, 32p. $16.95.

SUBJECTS: Automobiles—Fiction; Environmental protection—Fiction

This quirky picture book takes a look at one of the problems of American overpopulation—automobiles and society's dependence on them. In this tale, a grandfather restores a Model T as he tells his grandchildren "you gotta have wheels!" When they finally take the car out for a spin, it becomes clear that there are too many cars on the road and the children begin to ponder the problems caused by all these cars, including oil consumption and pollution. The text and illustrations are lively, colorful, and lighthearted, although the subject is serious and begs readers to find solutions to the questions posed in this book. 🌳

87   Ellerbee, Linda. *Girl Reporter Blows Lid Off Town.*
GRADES: 5—7
SERIES: GET REAL. HarperCollins, 2000, ISBN 978-0-06-028245-5,
195p. $14.89.
SUBJECTS: Pollution—Fiction; Journalism—Fiction

Sixth-grader Casey Smith hits the ground running at her new school, deciding to revive the school's newspaper. Unfortunately, the popular and
prissy Megan O'Connor has the same idea and the two have different plans
for the newspaper's content. Casey's first article leads her to investigate the
local paper mill and the pollution it is dumping into the river. 🌳

88   Farrelly, Peter. *Abigale the Happy Whale.*
GRADES: PS—2
Ill. by Jamie Rama. Little, Brown, 2006, ISBN 978-0-316-01190-7,
32p. $15.99.
SUBJECTS: Water pollution—Fiction; Humpback whale—Fiction;
Marine animals—Fiction

Abigale's happy disposition is tested when she realizes the effect that human
pollution has on her home, the ocean, and all of her ocean friends. Her
clever solution to this growing problem is to show the humans just how
much pollution is on the ocean floor and make them accept responsibility for
their own waste. Though the subject is no laughing matter, the story is cutely
told with lovable characters. Rama's bold, expressive illustrations are the
true heart of the story. 🌐 🌳

89   Gratz, Alan. *Something Rotten: A Horatio Wilkes Mystery.*
GRADES: 6—9
Dial Books, 2007, ISBN 978-0-8037-3216-2, 208p. $16.99.
SUBJECTS: Water pollution—Fiction

Take Shakespeare's Hamlet, turn him into a modern-day teenager, add some
corporate greed and pollution and you have *Something Rotten*. Those unfamiliar with the story of *Hamlet* (i.e., many teenage readers) will find this an
intriguing ecological murder mystery. Horatio Wilkes arrives in Denmark,
Tennessee, to visit his best friend from boarding school, Hamilton Prince.
Horatio is soon embroiled in a murder mystery surrounding the death of the
senior Prince as well as being enlisted to help Hamilton's ex-girlfriend Olivia

clean up the pollution of the Copenhagen River caused by the Princes' company—the Elsinore Paper Plant. Sound familiar? 🌳

---

90   Hiaasen, Carl. *Flush.*
GRADES: 4—6
Knopf, 2005, ISBN 978-0-375-82182-0, 272p. $16.95.
SUBJECTS: Environmental protection—Fiction; Water pollution—Fiction

When his dad ends up in jail for sinking the *Coral Queen,* a luxury casino boat, it's up to Noah to find out what is really going on. His dad claims that the owner of the *Coral Queen* has been dumping the boat's sewage into the harbor and that he had to sink the boat to stop it. It turns out that Noah's dad just may be on to something. Featuring a colorful cast of characters and Hiaasen's characteristic wit, this book is a crowd-pleaser with humor, mystery, and a heavy dose of social consciousness. 🌳

---

91   Johns, Linda. *Hannah West in Deep Water.*
GRADES: 3—6
SERIES: HANNAH WEST. Puffin, 2006, pap., ISBN 978-0-14-240700-4, 160p. $5.99.
SUBJECTS: Water pollution—Fiction; Mystery stories—Fiction

Hollywood excitement meets mystery intrigue in this installment in the Hannah West series. Twelve-year-old Hannah has just moved to Portage Bay when dead fish start washing ashore and a film crew sets up shop. She and her best friend, Lily Shannon, discover that pollution could be the culprit. This is a fast-moving, funny, and clever story that will delight young environmentalists (and budding movie stars!). 🌳

---

92   Petrucha, Stefan. *Teen, Inc.*
GRADES: 7—9
Walker and Co., 2007, ISBN 978-0-8027-9650-9, 244p. $16.95.
SUBJECTS: Business ethics—Fiction; Pollution—Fiction; High school—Fiction

When Jaiden was an infant, his parents were killed by defective equipment manufactured by NECorp. In an unprecedented turn of events, the company adopted him and treated him as a special project during his childhood and adolescence. NECorp becomes the only family Jaiden knows and he must make difficult decisions when he realizes NECorp may again be guilty of negligence—in this case, mercury poisoning. A clever, quick, and interesting read.

---

93   Quinn, Zoe. *Totally Toxic.*
GRADES: 3–6
SERIES: THE CAPED 6TH GRADER. Ill. by Brie Spangler. Yearling, 2006, ISBN 978-0-385-90305-9, 160p. $11.99.
SUBJECTS: Superheroes—Fiction; Water pollution—Fiction; Hazardous wastes—Fiction

In this installment in the series, superhero Zoe Richards uses her recently discovered powers to get to the bottom of a possible pollution predicament. Since Zoe isn't a full-fledged superhero yet, she has to keep her abilities secret, solve the mystery, and navigate all of the other problems facing adolescent girls: boys, school, and parents! A fun, quick read punctuated with graphic-novel-style illustrations, this book may not inspire, but it will entertain and will be a hit with girls. 🌳

---

94   Rowe, John A. *Moondog.*
GRADES: PS–2
Minedition, 2005, ISBN 978-0-698-40031-3, 32p.
SUBJECTS: Pollution—Fiction; Dogs—Fiction; Moon—Fiction

This clever little picture book introduces Moondog, a dog who—you got it— lives on the moon. He discovers that the people of the Earth want to move to the moon because they have polluted their own rivers, cut down the trees, and built too many buildings. Moondog hatches a plan to keep the moon bright and shiny and to force people to solve Earth's problems. Colorful, quirky illustrations dance across the pages to help tell this fantastical story. 🌳

---

95   Teitelbaum, Michael, adapt. *Dora Saves Mermaid Kingdom.*
GRADES: PS–2
SERIES: DORA THE EXPLORER. Ill. by Artful Doodlers. Simon Spotlight/Nick Jr., 2007, ISBN 978-1-4352-0980-0, 22p. $12.99.

SUBJECTS: Pollution—Fiction; Refuse and refuse disposal—Fiction; Mermaids—Fiction

Dora and Boots begin their day by picking up garbage on the beach and find themselves in the middle of a fairy tale about a mermaid land that is polluted by an evil octopus. Dora must help save the mermaid kingdom. Along the way, readers learn a few Spanish words, practice their counting, and use comprehension skills. While fictional and fantastical, this book is a good choice for young readers who are already fans of Dora, and helps introduce the ideas of pollution and conservation. ♣

96   Testa, Fulvio. *Too Much Garbage.*
GRADES: PS–2
Ill. by the author. North-South, 2001, ISBN 978-0-7358-1451-6, 32p.
SUBJECTS: Refuse and refuse disposal—Fiction; Pollution—Fiction

Tony's turn to take out the trash becomes an examination of the growing amount of garbage—on the streets, in the trees, and in the landfills. A solitary flower growing in a massive landfill inspires Tony and his friend to do something about this crisis. This book is an easy-to-read, simple look at a complex problem, with large text and illustrations. While it doesn't offer any solution to pollution, it can help start a conversation with very young readers about reducing the amount of garbage they produce. ♣

97   Ward, Helen. *Varmints.*
GRADES: PS–2
Ill. by Marc Craste. Candlewick Press, 2008, pap., ISBN 978-0-7636-3796-5, 32p. $12.99.
SUBJECTS: Conservation of natural resources—Fiction; Pollution—Fiction

Varmints is a visually stunning story of pollution and a cautionary tale about what happens when nature is taken for granted. One varmint remembers the sound of bees and nurtures his tiny piece of wilderness, hoping for a better future. This unique picture book has potential to be a read-aloud for young audiences, but may be difficult for young readers to tackle on their own as the text is integrated into the illustrations and is sometimes difficult to discern. Visually striking, this book is worth picking up for the illustrations alone but also carries a great message. ♣

98   Yolen, Jane. *Where Have the Unicorns Gone?*
GRADES: PS—2
Ill. by Ruth Sanderson. Simon & Schuster, 2000, ISBN 978-0-689-82465-4, 32p. $16.95.
SUBJECTS: Unicorns—Fiction; Environmental protection—Fiction

This beautiful picture book imagines a world where unicorns once roamed and thrived. Detailed and whimsical illustrations show the unicorns being forced to move further and further away from pollution until they finally find a home in the crashing waves of the sea. Yolen's lyrical, rhyming story combines with Sanderson's rich illustrations to create an ecological fairy tale sure to appeal to all ages. 🌳

WATCHING AND LISTENING GREEN

99   *Environmental Health: Health for Children.*
GRADES: K—4
DVD. Schlessinger Media, 2005, ISBN 978-1-4171-0114-6, $29.95. 23 minutes
SUBJECTS: Environmental health; Pollution; Recycling

Short segments on topics such as pollution, "health heroes," and recycling keep this short film moving along. Each segment provides information about pollution's causes and effects—and about how to create less of it. The youthful narrators and upbeat music help hold the interest of younger audiences. Includes a teacher's guide. ♻ 🌐

100   Miyazaki, Hayao. *Nausicaa of the Valley of the Wind.*
GRADES: 7—12
DVD. Walt Disney Home Entertainment, 2004, ISBN 978-0-7888-2400-5, $29.99. 117 minutes
SUBJECTS: Pollution—Fiction; Princesses—Fiction; Anime—Fiction

Touted as an "epic environmental cautionary tale," this movie was adapted from a graphic novel series. After an ecological disaster has destroyed most of the Earth's resources, empires fight over the remaining compromised materials. At the forefront of this series is Princess Nausicaa, who alone tries to restore ecological balance while uniting the empires. The graphic novel series will satisfy manga lovers and the animated film will delight anime fans. This is a great recommendation for young teens and for older readers. ♣

---

101 Stanton, Andrew, dir. *WALL-E*.
GRADES: PS**and up**
DVD. Walt Disney Home Entertainment, 2008, ISBN 978-0-7888-7693-6, $29.99. Writing Credits: Andrew Stanton, Pete Docter, and Jim Reardon; 98 minutes
SUBJECTS: Robots—Fiction; Refuse and refuse disposal—Fiction; Friendship—Fiction

This futuristic science fiction tale focuses on the adventures of WALL-E (Waste Allocation Load Lifter—Earth-Class), who spends his days cleaning up the waste left behind by humans. While WALL-E cleans up Earth, the increasingly lazy and wasteful race of humans is floating along in space. When another robot named EVE arrives on Earth, searching for signs of life, she and WALL-E strike up an unlikely friendship. This movie is a cautionary tale wrapped up in a sweet story of hope and romance that is fun for all ages. ♣

NONFICTION

102 Amsel, Sheri. *The Everything Kids' Environment Book: Learn How You Can Help Save the Environment—By Getting Involved at School, at Home, or at Play.*
GRADES: 6—8
SERIES: EVERYTHING KIDS. Adams Media, 2007, pap., ISBN 978-1-59869-670-7, 129p. $7.95.
SUBJECTS: Environmental protection; Pollution

The title of this interactive book is not misleading: it covers all aspects of the environment, including how our planet works, the importance of habitats, and how humans affect the environment. The text is small and could be intimidating, but the author covers a ton of subjects and sprinkles thirty puzzles throughout the book (librarians be warned: it begs to be written in). Packed with green-living tips and helpful definitions, this book is worth more than its price. ♻ 🌐 ♣

103   Baron, Robert, and Thomas Locker. *Hudson: Story of a River.*

GRADES: 2—4

Ill. by Thomas Locker. Fulcrum Publishing, 2004, ISBN 978-1-55591-512-4, 32p. $17.95.

SUBJECTS: Water pollution; Hudson River

The story of the Hudson River is told with a mix of imagination and fact. The nostalgic and reverent tone of the text is mirrored in the breathtaking full-page illustrations that help to tell the story of the river and the many changes (including pollution) it has endured over the years. This book will have a broad appeal to art, science, and history enthusiasts as well as to environmentalists. 🌳

104   Bellamy, Rufus. *Clean Air.*

GRADES: 4—6

SERIES: ACTION FOR THE ENVIRONMENT. Smart Apple Media, 2006, ISBN 978-1-58340-594-9, 32p. $27.10.

SUBJECTS: Air pollution; Air quality management

This book in the Action for the Environment series uses large, bold text and colorful pictures to enliven the content. The short chapters explore the issue of air pollution by explaining its causes and effects. "Action Stations" in every chapter provide examples of responsible and clever ways to improve the environment. ♻ 🌐

105   Bily, Cynthia A., ed. *Pollution.*

GRADES: 7—10

SERIES: INTRODUCING ISSUES WITH OPPOSING VIEWPOINTS. Greenhaven Press, 2006, ISBN 978-0-7377-3546-8, 144p. $33.70.

SUBJECTS: Pollution; Environmental protection; Opposing viewpoints

Aimed at a slightly younger reader than the Opposing Viewpoints series, this book presents a truly balanced perspective on pollution. By featuring brief, well-edited articles and examining many sides of the issue, it helps readers develop critical-thinking and research skills without using overly complicated language. Complementing the articles are color photographs, charts, and even cartoons. An annotated bibliography, comprehension questions, and fact boxes are also included. 🌐

106 Binns, Tristan Boyer. *Clean Planet: Stopping Litter and Pollution.*
GRADES: 3—5
SERIES: YOU CAN SAVE THE PLANET. Heinemann, 2005, ISBN 978-1-4034-6846-8, 32p. $19.75.
SUBJECTS: Pollution

Short, fact-filled paragraphs and bright contemporary pictures make this book easy to read. "Taking Action" boxes give the reader quick and easy ways to explore environmental activism and the "Science Behind It" boxes provide a better understanding of pollution. Also notable in this book are the case studies that give real-life, hands-on examples of how to reduce pollution, including an ultracool solar car race—sure to excite even the most diehard racing fans. ♻ ☻

107 Burns, Loree Griffin. *Tracking Trash: Flotsam, Jetsam, and the Science of Ocean Motion.*
GRADES: 5—8
SERIES: SCIENTISTS IN THE FIELD. Houghton Mifflin, 2007, ISBN 978-0-618-58131-3, 58p. $18.00.
SUBJECTS: Water pollution; Marine debris; Ocean currents

Oceanographer Curt Ebbesmeyer's curiosity is at the heart of this scientific book with an ecological message. It was his curiosity about the trash washing ashore near his home in Seattle that led him to explore how ocean currents carry objects, including trash. The easy and intriguing narrative will immediately draw in readers. The pictures, diagrams, glossary, and index make this a pleasurable read and a valuable research resource. ♻ ☻ ♣

Calhoun, Yael.
SERIES: ENVIRONMENTAL ISSUES. Chelsea House

108 *Air Quality.*
GRADES: 9—12
2005, ISBN 978-0-7910-8201-0, 164p. $31.95.
SUBJECTS: Air pollution; Air quality management

109 *Water Pollution.*
GRADES: 9—12
2005, ISBN 978-0-7910-8202-7, 164p. $31.95.
SUBJECTS: Water pollution

Each book in this series takes an in-depth look at an environmental issue and how it is related to other environmental concerns. These books use academic language and do not feature charts, graphics, or photographs. Each chapter includes articles written by different authors to provide varied perspectives. Bibliographies and extensive indexes add to this series' value as a research resource for high school collections. ♲ ◐

---

110 Challen, Paul. *Environmental Disaster Alert.*
GRADES: 3—6
SERIES: DISASTER ALERT! Crabtree Publishing, 2005, ISBN 978-0-7787-1581-8, 32p. $19.95.
SUBJECTS: Disasters—Environmental aspects; Environmental degradation

Despite its alarmist title (or perhaps because of it), this series appeals to children's natural curiosity about disasters. This book explores the causes of these disasters and what can be done to alleviate their effects. The short chapters—combined with bright graphics, diagrams, and photographs—add to this book's appeal. Also helpful are tips on how to avoid environmental disasters, a glossary, and an index. ◐

SERIES: YOUR CARBON FOOTPRINT. Rosen Publishing

111 David, Sarah B. *Reducing Your Carbon Footprint at Home.*
GRADES: 4—7
2008, ISBN 978-1-4042-1772-0, 48p. $26.50.
SUBJECTS: Energy conservation; Atmospheric carbon dioxide; Water conservation; Recycling

112 Furgang, Kathy, and Adam Furgang. *On the Move: Green Transportation.*
GRADES: 4—7
2008, ISBN 978-1-4042-1773-7, 48p. $26.50.
SUBJECTS: Transportation—Environmental aspects; Atmospheric carbon dioxide

113 Hall, Linley Erin. *Reducing Your Carbon Footprint in the Kitchen.*
GRADES: 4—7
2008, ISBN 978-1-4042-1776-8, 48p. $26.50.
SUBJECTS: Organic living; Environmental responsibility; Water conservation

114 Nagle, Jeanne. *Reducing Your Carbon Footprint at School.*
GRADES: 4—7
2008, ISBN 978-1-4042-1774-4, 48p. $26.50.
SUBJECTS: Automobiles—Environmental aspects; School—Energy conservation; Atmospheric carbon dioxide

115 Nagle, Jeanne. *Smart Shopping: Shopping Green.*
GRADES: 4—7
2009, ISBN 978-1-4042-1775-1, 48p. $26.50.
SUBJECTS: Consumer education; Sustainable living; Environmental protection

116 Roza, Greg. *Reducing Your Carbon Footprint on Vacation.*
GRADES: 4—7
2008, ISBN 978-1-4042-1777-5, 48p. $26.50.
SUBJECTS: Ecotourism; Sustainable living; Energy conservation

This new series is devoted entirely to helping children lower their carbon footprint! Each volume begins by explaining what our carbon footprint is and how it affects the environment. Stocked with practical tips that ask children to evaluate their actions in the kitchen, at school, and even on vacation, this is a great series for motivated children! Each book includes a comprehensive glossary, a bibliography, and an index. ♻ ❸

117 Day, Trevor. *Water.*
GRADES: 3—6
SERIES: SEE FOR YOURSELF. DK Publishing, 2007, ISBN 978-0-7566-2562-7, 64p. $14.99.
SUBJECTS: Water pollution; Hydroelectricity energy resources

Do not be fooled by the fact that the books in this series look like picture books—they pack a scientific punch. Unique layouts, colorful photography, and informative captions help the reader to fully understand water as a resource before explaining how pollution and global warming affect it. Younger readers will be drawn in by the design of the book and older readers will respect the large amount of information in its pages. ❸

Desonie, Dana.
SERIES: OUR FRAGILE PLANET. Chelsea House

118 *Atmosphere: Air Pollution and Its Effects.*
GRADES: 6—12

2007, ISBN 978-0-8160-6213-3, 194p. $35.00.
SUBJECTS: Atmosphere; Air pollution

119 *Humans and the Natural Environment: The Future of Our Planet.*
GRADES: 6–12
2008, ISBN 978-0-8160-6220-1, 194p. $35.00.
SUBJECTS: Environmental degradation; Nature—Effect of human
beings on; Human ecology

120 *Hydrosphere: Freshwater Systems and Pollution.*
GRADES: 6–12
2007, ISBN 978-0-8160-6215-7, 194p. $35.00.
SUBJECTS: Water pollution

121 *Oceans: How We Use the Sea.*
GRADES: 6–12
2007, ISBN 978-0-8160-6216-4, 194p. $35.00.
SUBJECTS: Water pollution; Marine ecology

Four books in the Our Fragile Planet series address the impact that humans
are having on the atmosphere, hydrosphere, oceans, and habitats. The books
in this series are structured very much like middle school textbooks in both
appearance and content. Photographs, charts, and diagrams combine with
vocabulary words in bold type, a glossary, and an index to add to the textbook feel. The effect is a comprehensive look at each global issue in a format
familiar to middle school students. This series is recommended for the serious environmental researcher. ♺ ◉

122 Dorion, Christine. *Earth's Garbage Crisis.*
GRADES: 5–7
SERIES: WHAT IF WE DO NOTHING? World Almanac Library, 2007, ISBN
978-0-8368-7753-3, 48p. $31.00.
SUBJECTS: Refuse and refuse disposal; Pollution

Each chapter in this book begins with a glimpse into a hypothetical future
in which nothing has been done to reduce the waste we produce. The chapters then explore the causes and effects of pollution and the steps that we can
take to prevent the waste crisis from escalating. Plainly written text, fast
facts, charts, tables, photographs, a glossary, and an index are all features of
this book. Theoretical questions sprinkled throughout ask the reader to consider environmental problems and their solutions. Answers are provided in
the back of the book. ♺ ◉

123 Faust, Daniel R. *Sinister Sludge: Oil Spills and the Environment.*

GRADES: 3–6

SERIES: JR. GRAPHIC ENVIRONMENTAL DANGERS. PowerKids Press, 2009, ISBN 978-1-4042-4597-6, 24p. $23.95.

SUBJECTS: Energy resources; Fossil fuels; Oil spills

This book in the Jr. Graphic Environmental Dangers series uses a graphic-novel format to address the problem of oil spills. The environmental crisis is illustrated through an exciting story that is based on fact. Equal parts entertainment and education, this series is good for reluctant readers and for children who need a nudge to get them started on their research. ❂ 🌳

124 Friedman, Lauri S., ed. *Writing the Critical Essay: Pollution.*

GRADES: 7–12

SERIES: AN OPPOSING VIEWPOINTS GUIDE. Greenhaven Press, 2007, ISBN 978-0-7377-3198-9, 130p. $29.95.

SUBJECTS: Pollution; Pollution—Health aspects; Opposing viewpoints; Opposing viewpoints

In the tradition of the Opposing Viewpoints series, the Opposing Viewpoints Guide series helps students evaluate and write critical essays. The first section of *Pollution* presents brief, well-written articles with contrasting perspectives on pollution. The second and third sections provide writing examples, pollution facts, and tools to prompt thoughtful research and evaluation of the topic. A wise choice for middle and high school collections. ❂

125 Gerdes, Louise, ed. *Endangered Oceans.*

GRADES: 9–12

SERIES: OPPOSING VIEWPOINTS. Greenhaven Press, 2008, ISBN 978-0-7377-4210-7, 234p. $37.40.

SUBJECTS: Marine resources conservation; Water pollution; Ocean—Environmental aspects; Opposing viewpoints

Coral reef destruction, overfishing, and governmental regulations are some of the controversial topics covered in this entry in the Opposing Viewpoints series. Brief articles, comprehension questions, and lists of additional resources help take the guesswork out of research. ❂

....

126 Gerdes, Louise, ed. *Pollution.*
GRADES: 9—12
SERIES: OPPOSING VIEWPOINTS. Greenhaven Press, 2006, ISBN 978-0-7377-2949-8, 221p. $37.40.
SUBJECTS: Pollution; Pollution prevention; Opposing viewpoints

Geared for high school students, this book in the Opposing Viewpoint series follows the tradition of its predecessors and presents many different sides of the issue of pollution. Articles about different types of pollution and differing opinions about the threat pollution poses to the environment provide students with a multileveled understanding of the issue. The annotated bibliography and comprehension questions provide further fodder for research. ◉

....

Gifford, Clive.
SERIES: PLANET UNDER PRESSURE. Heinemann

127 *Pollution.*
GRADES: 6—8
2006, ISBN 978-1-4034-7742-2, 48p. $22.00.
SUBJECTS: Pollution; Refuse and refuse disposal

128 *Waste.*
GRADES: 6—8
2006, ISBN 978-1-4034-7745-3, 48p. $22.00.
SUBJECTS: Refuse and refuse disposal

Gifford examines how waste and pollution are putting a tremendous strain on the earth, air, and water in these two books in the Planet Under Pressure series. The books focus first on the problems created by waste and pollution and then explore the solutions, using photographs, timely facts and figures, charts, and diagrams to thoroughly examine the topics. "What Do You Think?" and "What Can You Do?" boxes help children get involved with the material. ✾ ◉

....

129 Graham, Ian. *Air: A Resource Our World Depends On.*
GRADES: 3—5
SERIES: MANAGING OUR RESOURCES. Heinemann, 2005, ISBN 978-1-4034-5614-4, 32p. $28.21.
SUBJECTS: Air pollution

This book in the Managing Our Resources series focuses on air as a resource. The last few chapters focus on the impact of pollution on air and how air is affected by global warming. The layout moves the reader along, with "Do You Know?" text boxes providing quick facts and case studies that take a closer look at special subjects such as wind farms and submersibles. 🌐

130 Green, Jen. *Reducing Air Pollution.*
GRADES: 3–5
SERIES: IMPROVING OUR ENVIRONMENT. Gareth Stevens Publishing, 2005, ISBN 978-0-8368-4428-3, 32p. $19.50.
SUBJECTS: Air pollution; Air quality management

Descriptive text combines with large photographs and bold design to make this book about the causes and dangers of air pollution accessible to beginning readers. Fact boxes and experiments provide statistical information and hands-on experiences to engage the reader. The glossary, index, and bibliography are valuable tools for research. ♺ 🌐

131 Green, Robert. *Pollution.*
GRADES: 4–8
SERIES: GLOBAL PERSPECTIVES. Cherry Lake Publishing, 2008, ISBN 978-1-60279-130-5, 32p. $18.95.
SUBJECTS: Pollution

This book is ideal for readers who are reluctant to read nonfiction. The subject of pollution is anecdotally introduced through a conversation among students from many different countries. The students ask questions that prompt each chapter. The scientific information is accurate and relevant but accessible to even the most hesitant readers. 🌐

132 Guillain, Charlotte. *Cleaning Up Litter.*
GRADES: PS–2
SERIES: HELP THE ENVIRONMENT. Heinemann, 2008, ISBN 978-1-4329-0885-0, 24p. $20.71.
SUBJECTS: Pollution

Using simple words and repetitive phrases, this book helps children recognize ecological terms, become more environmentally conscious, and learn to read. The text is large and easy to read and is accompanied by photographs of children cleaning up litter. The simple picture glossary and index introduce young readers to research tools. ♺ ♟

---

133 Hirschmann, Kris. *Pollution*.
GRADES: 3–6
SERIES: OUR ENVIRONMENT. Kidhaven Press, 2004, ISBN 978-0-7377-1563-7, 48p. $26.20.
SUBJECTS: Pollution; Refuse and refuse disposal

The problems posed by different types of pollution, as well as possible solutions to these problems, are the focus of this book in the Our Environment series. Using rich illustrations, photographs, and vocabulary terms, *Pollution* describes how humans generate pollution and how pollution in turn affects humans. This comprehensive look at the issue includes a glossary, index, and bibliography. ❸

SERIES: SCIENCE MATTERS. Weigl Publishers

134 Hudak, Heather C. *Air Pollution*.
GRADES: 2–4
2007, ISBN 978-1-59036-415-4, 24p. $24.45.
SUBJECTS: Air pollution

135 Ostopowich, Melanie. *Water Pollution*.
GRADES: 2–4
2006, ISBN 978-1-59036-307-2, 24p. $24.45.
SUBJECTS: Water pollution

The Science Matters series provides an introductory look into current science topics. The design draws the reader in and the clear text makes the books easy to read. These titles engage the reader with questions, experiments, and environmental tips. The quick pace and interesting subjects make this series a good choice for struggling and reluctant readers interested in science. ♺ ❸

---

136 Inskipp, Carol. *Healthy Seas*.
GRADES: 2–4
SERIES: SUSTAINABLE FUTURES. Smart Apple Media, 2006, ISBN 978-1-58340-980-0, 48p. $31.35.
SUBJECTS: Water pollution; Marine ecology; Endangered ecosystems

Information about threats to the world's oceans is balanced by positive details of efforts to prevent water pollution in the future. Using plenty of color photographs, statistical charts, and case studies, the books in the Sustainable Futures series clearly explain global concerns and their solutions. Question-and-answer sections help the reader navigate through the lengthy text that educates about the impact of pollution on ocean life. ♼ ◐

---

137 Jakab, Cheryl. *Clean Air and Water.*
GRADES: 3—6
SERIES: GLOBAL ISSUES. Smart Apple Media, 2008, ISBN 978-1-59920-122-1, 32p. $27.10.
SUBJECTS: Air pollution; Water pollution

The importance of clean air and water is introduced to young readers in a highly accessible way in this book in the Global Issues series. It addresses each issue by providing examples of a global problem (such as air pollution) followed by possible solutions. This helps students understand the causes and effects of pollution while giving them a better understanding of and perspective on the impact of their everyday actions. The dynamic design adds interest to this valuable resource. ◐

---

138 Jakab, Cheryl. *Overpopulation.*
GRADES: 3—6
SERIES: GLOBAL ISSUES. Smart Apple Media, 2008, ISBN 978-1-59920-127-6, 32p. $27.10.
SUBJECTS: Overpopulation

Overpopulation can be a difficult concept for younger readers to grasp. This book features examples to explain the environmental impacts of overpopulation, which include (but are not limited to) pollution. Scientific information and case studies give the reader a more robust understanding of overpopulation. Appealing design, bright illustrations, and clear language make the information accessible. ◐

---

139 Kelly, D. D. *Radioactive Waste: Hidden Dangers.*
GRADES: 7—12
SERIES: EXTREME ENVIRONMENTAL THREATS. Rosen Publishing, 2007, ISBN 978-1-4042-0745-5, 64p. $29.25.
SUBJECTS: Radioactive waste disposal in the ground

Part of the Extreme Environmental Threats series, *Radioactive Waste* explores the cause and nature of radioactive waste as well as its serious dangers. While geared toward students in grades 7–12, the layout and length will appeal to younger audiences or to older students with lower reading skills. Research tools include tables, fast facts, color photographs, an extensive bibliography, a glossary, and an index. 🌐

---

140 Knight, M. J. *Why Shouldn't I Drop Litter?*
GRADES: 2–4
SERIES: ONE SMALL STEP. Smart Apple Media, 2009, ISBN 978-1-59920-265-5, 32p. $27.10.
SUBJECTS: Refuse and refuse disposal; Pollution

The two-page spreads in this book feature short, easy-to-read paragraphs, color photographs, and illustrations. Every spread includes "I Can Make a Difference" boxes with environmental tips and "One Small Fact" bubbles with quick scientific or statistical information about the importance of not polluting. Each book in this series has a glossary, Web resources, and an index. A very useful resource for impressing the importance of conservation upon young readers. ♻ 🌐

---

141 MacFarlane, Katherine. *Pesticides.*
GRADES: 3–6
SERIES: OUR ENVIRONMENT. Kidhaven Press, 2007, ISBN 978-0-7377-3619-9, 48p. $26.20.
SUBJECTS: Pesticides

Photographs, graphics, and fact boxes provide an in-depth look at the subject of pesticides. By explaining pesticides' use, their cost to the environment, and their alternatives, this book gives readers a well-rounded understanding of this controversial topic. Students can continue their research using the multimedia bibliography. 🌐

---

142 Mason, Paul. *Population.*
GRADES: 6–8
SERIES: PLANET UNDER PRESSURE. Heinemann, 2006, ISBN 978-1-4034-7741-5, 48p. $22.00.
SUBJECTS: Overpopulation; Natural resources

Mason answers the question "How is population growth threatening the earth's natural resources?" in *Population*. Readers will be challenged to think for themselves by the "What Do You Think?" and "What Can You Do?" sidebar features in this book. Part of the Planet Under Pressure series. ♻ ⊕

....

143 Miller, Debra A., ed. *Pollution*.
GRADES: 7–12
SERIES: CURRENT CONTROVERSIES. Greenhaven Press, 2008, pap., ISBN 978-0-7377-3728-8, 219p. $25.95.
SUBJECTS: Pollution

The Current Controversies series uses brief, age-appropriate, and varied articles in comprehensive examinations of controversial subjects. In *Pollution*, articles address issues including the causes and effects of pollution and the relationships between industry and pollution. A list of subject-related organizations, a bibliography, and an index are included. ⊕

....

Morgan, Sally.
SERIES: DEALING WITH WASTE. Smart Apple Media

144 *Household Waste*.
GRADES: 1–3
2008, ISBN 978-1-59920-008-8, 30p. $27.10.
SUBJECTS: Refuse and refuse disposal; Recycling

145 *Leftover Food*.
GRADES: 1–3
2008, ISBN 978-1-59920-009-5, 30p. $27.10.
SUBJECTS: Agricultural wastes; Composting

146 *Old Appliances*.
GRADES: 1–3
2008, ISBN 978-1-59920-012-5, 30p. $27.10.
SUBJECTS: Recycling; Waste electronic appliances

147 *Old Cars*.
GRADES: 1–3
2008, ISBN 978-1-59920-010-1, 30p. $27.10.
SUBJECTS: Automobiles—Recycling; Recycling

148 *Wastewater.*

GRADES: 1–3

2008, ISBN 978-1-59920-013-2, 30p. $27.10.

SUBJECTS: Water purification; Sewage—Purification

Disposing of waste can be difficult and harmful to the environment. Each book in this series considers a type of waste and looks at whether it can be recycled and how much pollution it causes. The importance of reducing waste and recycling everything possible is emphasized. Using colorful photographs and text boxes that draw attention to the waste in everyone's world, the series draws in young readers. Each book includes a glossary, a bibliography, an index, and useful tips for reducing, reusing, and recycling.

149 Morgan, Sally. *Waste and Recycling.*

GRADES: 2–4

SERIES: SUSTAINABLE FUTURES. Smart Apple Media, 2007, ISBN 978-1-58340-981-7, 48p. $31.35.

SUBJECTS: Refuse and refuse disposal; Recycling

An excellent choice for introducing children to the ideas of waste and recycling, this book also helps them realize that the choices they make could have a global impact. The color photographs, statistical charts, question-and-answer sections, and case studies found in each book in the Sustainable Futures series help to explain global concerns and their solutions. ♻ 🌐

Parks, Peggy J.
SERIES: OUR ENVIRONMENT. Kidhaven Press

150 *Acid Rain.*

GRADES: 3–6

2005, ISBN 978-0-7377-2628-2, 48p. $26.20.

SUBJECTS: Acid rain; Hazardous wastes; Oil spills; Water pollution

151 *Oil Spills.*

GRADES: 3–6

2005, ISBN 978-0-7377-2629-9, 48p. $26.20.

SUBJECTS: Oil spills

152 *Toxic Waste.*
GRADES: 3–6
2006, ISBN 978-0-7377-1823-2, 48p. $26.20.
SUBJECTS: Hazardous wastes

153 *Water Pollution.*
GRADES: 3–6
2007, ISBN 978-0-7377-3667-0, 48p. $26.20.
SUBJECTS: Water pollution

In this series, Parks examines the causes of acid rain, oil spills, toxic waste, and water pollution, as well as their effects and possible solutions. The issues are thoroughly examined using colorful diagrams, photographs, and definitions. Other helpful features in these books are the notes, multimedia bibliographies, glossaries, and indexes. ●

154 Povey, Karen D. *Garbage.*
GRADES: 3–6
SERIES: OUR ENVIRONMENT. Kidhaven Press, 2006, ISBN 978-0-7377-3558-1, 48p. $26.20.
SUBJECTS: Refuse and refuse disposal

Children are often enchanted with the subject of this book. Using accessible language, photographs, and explanations, this book will draw in even those who are not fans of garbage. It describes how we affect our environment when we produce waste—and how our environment affects us in return. A helpful tool for environmental research and a good recommendation for reluctant readers. ●

155 Price, Sean. *Water Pollution.*
GRADES: 2–4
SERIES: SAVING OUR WORLD. Marshall Cavendish, 2008, ISBN 978-0-7614-3221-0, 32p. $28.50.
SUBJECTS: Water pollution; Environmentalism

Large, dramatic photographs are the focus of the two-page layouts in this book in the Saving Our World series. The text uses comprehension questions and environmental tips to engage the reader while delivering information about the causes of water pollution and the impact it has on marine and freshwater systems. ♻ ●

....

156   Rapp, Valerie. *Protecting Earth's Air Quality.*
GRADES: 3—5
SERIES: SAVING OUR LIVING EARTH. Lerner Publishing, 2009, ISBN 978-0-8225-7558-0, 71p. $30.60.
SUBJECTS: Air pollution; Air quality management

Rapp provides a look at the problem of air pollution and the efforts being made to control it. Readers will learn of historical events, including legislation, that have affected the amount of pollution in the air. Real children and young adults working to improve the environment are featured throughout the book in pictures and in the text. The detailed text, rich layout, bold photographs, bibliography, index, and glossary are nice features that are included in all the books in the Saving Our Living Earth series. ♻ ⊕

....

157   Rose, Elizabeth. *Human Impact on the Environment.*
GRADES: 2—4
SERIES: LIFE SCIENCE LIBRARY. PowerKids Press, 2006, ISBN 978-1-4042-2822-1, 24p. $21.25.
SUBJECTS: Human ecology; Nature—Effect of human beings on; Pollution

Two-page spreads feature large, easy-to-read text on one side and color photographs on the other. The text provides a basic introduction to the impact that humans have on the environment, including examples of degradation and conservation. Also included in this beginning reader are fact boxes, a glossary, and an index. ♻ ⊕

....

Royston, Angela.
SERIES: PROTECT OUR PLANET. Heinemann

158   *Oceans and Rivers in Danger.*
GRADES: K—2
2008, ISBN 978-1-4329-0926-0, 32p. $25.36.
SUBJECTS: Endangered ecosystems; Water pollution

159   *Polluted Air.*
GRADES: K—2
2008, ISBN 978-1-4329-0925-3, 32p. $25.36.
SUBJECTS: Air pollution; Atmosphere

The first half of both books explores the problems of air and water pollution using large text, vocabulary words in bold type, charts, maps, and descriptive photographs. The second half uses the same tactics to feature ways in which humans are beginning to protect natural resources, including both global and individual efforts that young readers may want to re-create. Each book includes a glossary, index, and multimedia bibliography. ♺ ●

160 Sechrist, Darren. *Air Pollution.*
GRADES: 2–4
SERIES: SAVING OUR WORLD. Marshall Cavendish, 2008, ISBN 978-0-7614-3220-3, 32p. $28.50.
SUBJECTS: Air pollution; Environmentalism

Information about the scientific and social aspects of air pollution, helpful environmental tips, and comprehension questions make this a useful book. Large, dramatic photographs are the focus of two-page layouts that examine specific causes of pollution. The eye-catching design overwhelms the text, but this is still a high-quality resource for any environmental collection. ♺ ●

161 Spilsbury, Louise. *Environment at Risk: The Effects of Pollution.*
GRADES: 3–6
SERIES: GEOGRAPHY FOCUS. Raintree Publishers, 2006, ISBN 978-1-4109-1113-1, 48p. $31.43.
SUBJECTS: Pollution; Environmental protection

Photographs, diagrams, and charts keep the reader's attention while covering the negative effects that pollution has on the environment. Each two-page spread uses short, information-packed paragraphs and "fast fact" boxes to convey ideas succinctly. Vocabulary words, a glossary, a bibliography, and an index add to the value of this book. Attractive, dynamic, and contemporary, this book is part of the Geography Focus series. ●

162 Stefanow, Jennifer. *Polluted Waters.*
GRADES: 2–4
SERIES: GREEN ALERT! Raintree Publishers, 2004, ISBN 978-1-84421-663-5, 48p. $31.43.
SUBJECTS: Water pollution

This book in the Green Alert! series provides an in-depth look at water pollution, at who generates it, and at what is being done about it. Diagrams and large color photographs supplement the text. Case studies help illustrate the urgent need to protect water sources from pollution, and practical tips give readers ideas on ways to assist in the effort. Includes a glossary, an index, and a bibliography. ✿ ⊕

163 Stewart, Gail B. *Pollution.*
GRADES: 3–5
SERIES: RIPPED FROM THE HEADLINES: THE ENVIRONMENT. Erickson, 2008, ISBN 978-1-60217-026-1, 64p. $23.95.
SUBJECTS: Overpopulation—Environmental aspects; Pollution

Despite the rather dramatic series title, this is a balanced look at the problem of pollution using charts, environmental vocabulary, photographs, and science concepts. Well-documented quotations from a wide range of sources make this series unique. Includes a bibliography and an index. ⊕

164 Trapp, Clayton. *Polluted Air.*
GRADES: 2–4
SERIES: GREEN ALERT! Raintree Publishers, 2004, ISBN 978-0-7398-7011-2, 48p. $31.43.
SUBJECTS: Air pollution

Bright photographs and brief chapters help keep readers interested in the causes and effects of air pollution. Each chapter explores a different aspect of the subject, providing children with a rich introduction to this global concern. Other tools include case studies, environmental tips, a glossary, an index, and a bibliography. ✿ ⊕

165 Walker, Pam, and Elaine Wood. *People and the Sea.*
GRADES: 6–12
SERIES: LIFE IN THE SEA. Facts on File, 2005, ISBN 978-0-8160-5706-1, 132p. $35.

SUBJECTS: Water pollution; Oceanography

People and the Sea is all about the relationship between humans and the oceans—and the often-disastrous effects that humans have on the seas. Mostly black-and-white illustrations, charts, and diagrams give this book the feel of a textbook (although there are six pages of color photographs). The substance of the book is in the text, which covers subjects including commercial fishing, marine pollution, global warming, and nutrients in the ocean. Includes a glossary and a comprehensive index. ◐

166   Watson, Stephanie, ed. *Critical Perspectives on Pollution.*
GRADES: 9–12
SERIES: SCIENTIFIC AMERICAN CRITICAL ANTHOLOGIES ON ENVIRONMENT AND CLIMATE. Rosen Publishing, 2006, ISBN 978-1-4042-0690-8, 224p. $31.95.
SUBJECTS: Pollution

The books in this series consist of collections of *Scientific American* articles originally published between 1995 and 2005 that relate to energy and power resources. Most of the articles include black-and-white graphics such as diagrams, charts, and illustrations to complement the text. High school students will find these useful for reports, debates, or speeches about the causes and effects of pollution. ◐

167   Woods, Michael, and Mary B. Woods. *Environmental Disasters.*
GRADES: 4–6
SERIES: DISASTERS UP CLOSE. Lerner Publishing, 2007, ISBN 978-0-8225-6774-5, 64p. $27.93.
SUBJECTS: Environmental disasters; Hazardous substances—Accidents

Part of the Disasters Up Close series, this book examines the causes and effects of environmental disasters. It also investigates how events such as chemical spills and nuclear accidents can be avoided and how they are cleaned up. Descriptive photographs and informative text boxes accentuate the book's colorful design and illustrate the importance of regulating environmentally hazardous material. ◐

RECYCLED FAVORITES

168 Asch, Frank. *The Earth and I.*
GRADES: PS–2
Ill. by the author. Gulliver Green, 1994, ISBN 978-0-15-200443-9, 32p. $15.00.
SUBJECTS: Pollution—Fiction

Asch uses soft watercolor illustrations to show the relationship between a young boy and his environment. The text and illustrations combine to explain that pollution makes the world sad and cleaning up the Earth makes the world happy. The book uses concepts and emotions that young children can identify with and simple, short sentences perfect for the youngest readers. 🌳

Berenstain, Stan, and Jan Berenstain.
SERIES: BERENSTAIN BEARS.

169 *The Berenstain Bear Scouts and the Coughing Catfish.*
GRADES: 2–4
Scholastic, 1995, pap., ISBN 978-0-590-60384-3, 99p. $3.99.
SUBJECTS: Pollution—Fiction; Conservation of natural resources—Fiction; Bears—Fiction

170 *The Berenstain Bears Don't Pollute (Anymore).*
GRADES: PS–2
Scholastic, 1991, ISBN 978-0-679-92351-0, 32p.
SUBJECTS: Pollution—Fiction; Conservation of natural resources—Fiction; Bears—Fiction

The Berenstain Bears take on pollution and conservation in these recycled favorites. Brother and Sister Bear study ecology and conservation with the help of Professor Actual Factual. Together with their community, the Bears come up with some helpful ways to save their environment. *The Berenstain Bear Scouts and the Coughing Catfish* is a beginning chapter book and *The Berenstain Bears Don't Pollute (Anymore)* is for younger readers. 🌳

171 Bodecker, N. M. *The Mushroom Center Disaster.*
GRADES: 3–5

Ill. by Erik Blegvad. MacAdam/Cage Children's Books, 1974, ISBN 978-1-931561-98-3, 42p. $19.00.
SUBJECTS: Pollution—Fiction; Recycling—Fiction; Insects—Fiction

"To you, perhaps, the remains of a picnic dropped somewhere in the woods doesn't mean much. But a mess is a mess, and to the people in Mushroom Center, this mess was a disaster." That is because the people of Mushroom Center are crickets, ladybugs, snails, and moths. This charming tale is punctuated by delicate pen-and-ink drawings and is every bit as relevant today as the bugs learn to turn human waste into recycled resources. 🌳

172 MacGregor, Ellen, and Dora Pantell. *Miss Pickerell and the Supertanker.*
GRADES: 5—8
Ill. by Charles Geer. McGraw-Hill, 1978, ISBN 978-0-07-044588-8, 157p.
SUBJECTS: Oil pollution—Fiction

Ellen MacGregor's beloved classic character Miss Pickerell was ahead of her time in this environmental tale. When Miss Pickerell discovers that the supertanker she is vacationing on is killing sea life, she takes matters into her own hands. The black-and-white illustrations portray a harried and active Miss Pickerell with aplomb. While dated, this book is a sweet, classic tale with a big heart. 🌳

173 Wildsmith, Brian. *Professor Noah's Spaceship.*
GRADES: PS—2
Ill. by the author. Star Bright Books, 1980, ISBN 978-1-59572-124-2, 32p. $16.95.
SUBJECTS: Pollution—Fiction; Ecology—Fiction

This book parallels the Noah's Ark story and is driven by the extraordinary illustrations. The animals of Earth are troubled by the effects of pollution and deforestation and head into space on Professor Noah's spaceship in search of a better planet. The science fiction story is a tad too whimsical to be effective, but stands out because of Wildsmith's artful and surreal illustrations. 🌳

"THE LORAX"

Originally published in 1971, this classic environmental cautionary tale is often one of the first that comes to mind when searching for "green" material for kids. Dr. Seuss's inventive text and illustrations tell the tale of Truffula Trees, the Brown Bar-ba-loots, and the Lorax—the voice of the trees. The lyrical, often tongue-twisting text provides a fantastical look at the all-too-real problems of consumerism, pollution, overpopulation, environmental degradation, and greed. Adult environmentalists love the book for its message, but kids love it for all the reasons they love Dr. Seuss: the funny words, the rhymes, and the silly illustrations. Still widely available in book form, it is also available in DVD and audiobook. All formats are still highly recommended as timeless tools to build a more environmentally conscious audience.

174 Seuss, Dr. *The Lorax.*
GRADES: PS–2
SERIES: CLASSIC SEUSS. Ill. by the author. Random House, 1971, ISBN 978-0-394-82337-9, 72p. $14.95.
SUBJECTS: Environmental protection—Fiction; Deforestation—Fiction; Pollution—Fiction; Nature conservation—Fiction 🌳

175 Seuss, Dr. *Oh, the Places You'll Go! The Lorax.*
GRADES: PS–2
Audiobook on CD. Random House/Listening Library, 2007, ISBN 978-0-7393-6391-1, $9.99. Read by Ted Danson
SUBJECTS: Environmental protection—Fiction; Deforestation—Fiction; Pollution—Fiction; Nature conservation—Fiction 🌳

176 Pratt, Hawley, dir. *The Lorax/Pontoffel Pock and His Magic Piano.*
GRADES: PS–2
DVD. SERIES: ANIMATED TELEVISED CLASSICS. Universal Studios, 2003, $9.99. Starring: Eddie Albert, Bob Holy, Athena Lorde, Harlen Carraher
SUBJECTS: Environmental protection—Fiction; Deforestation—Fiction; Pollution—Fiction; Nature conservation—Fiction 🌳

177 Pratt, Hawley, dir. *Seuss Celebration: The Grinch Grinches the Cat in the Hat/The Cat in the Hat/Green Eggs and Ham/The Lorax.*
GRADES: PS–2

DVD. SERIES: ANIMATED TELEVISED CLASSICS. Universal Studios, 2005, ISBN 978-1-4170-6902-6, $26.98. Starring: Eddie Albert, Bob Holy, Athena Lorde, Harlen Carraher
SUBJECTS: Environmental protection—Fiction; Deforestation—Fiction; Pollution—Fiction; Nature conservation—Fiction 🌳

POLLUTION STORYTIME

Begin with "Good Morning, Dear Earth."

Good morning, dear Earth
Good morning, dear Sun (hold your hands above your head)
Good morning, dear stones (put a "stone" in your hand)
And the flowers, every one. (make your hand into a flower)

Good morning, dear bees (fly a "bee" around between your fingers)
And the birds in the trees (make your arms into wings and flap them)
Good morning to you (point to the children)
And good morning to me. (point to yourself)

"Good morning, children. Today we are going to talk—and read stories—about a very messy thing called pollution."

Hold up a tissue, "sneeze" into it, and drop it on the ground.

"When you use a tissue, what do you do when you are finished with it? Do you drop it on the ground? What would happen if everyone threw his or her garbage on the ground? Let's read a story about pollution to find out."

Read *Trash Trouble* by Larry Dane Brimner (see entry 85).

"We can clean up garbage just like the Corner Kids did!"

Sprinkle paper scraps around the room and, as you sing, walk around with a trash bin that the children can put the scraps in.

Sing "We Don't Pollute" (to the tune of "Ten Little Indians").

Picking up trash, and putting it in the garbage
Picking up trash, and putting it in the garbage
Picking up trash, and putting it in the garbage
Because we don't pollute!

Repeat until all the scraps are picked up.

"Unfortunately, people pollute everywhere! Our cars pollute the air and some people pollute the water, like the ocean. Do you know any animals that live in the ocean? What is the largest animal living in the ocean? We're going to read a story about a clever little whale named Abigale."

Read *Abigale, the Happy Whale* by Peter Farrelly (see entry 88).

"I know a fun activity that doesn't pollute: Dancing! Let's stand up and dance to a song about trash!"

Play the Chris McKhool song called "No More Trash!" (see entry 430).

"If we clean up the Earth and don't pollute, we will make the Earth very happy."

Read *The Earth and I* by Frank Asch (see entry 168).

"I want to make the Earth happy, so I will not pollute and I will pick up trash that I see on the ground and put it where it belongs—in the recycling or garbage bin."

Sing "In the Garbage" (to the tune of "Frère Jacques").

> *In the garbage, in the garbage,*
> *Put your trash, put your trash,*
> *This will make the Earth glad,*
> *This will make the Earth glad,*
> *In the garbage, put your trash.*

"Sneeze" into a tissue again.

"What should I do with this tissue? That's right, throw it in the garbage. I hope you remember to do that too!"

Sing "If You Love Earth and You Know It" (to the tune of "If You're Happy and You Know It").

> *If you love Earth and you know it, clap your hands!*
> *If you love Earth and you know it, clap your hands!*
> *If you love Earth and you know it, then let your actions show it!*
> *If you love Earth and you know it, clap your hands!*
>
> *Second verse: If you love Earth and you know it, stomp your feet!*

Third verse: If you love Earth and you know it, shout "Reduce!"
If you love Earth and you know it, shout "Reuse!"
If you love Earth and you know it, then let your actions show it!
If you love Earth and you know it, shout "Recycle!"

EARTH'S
RESOURCES

ENERGY RESOURCES ARE CONFUSING. How can wind and water
be harnessed to produce electricity? Even adults find the science difficult. But children need to understand the importance of energy and natural
resources in order to develop respect for them.

The most basic books in this area help children identify the natural resources around them. Then children can begin to comprehend how those resources are used and why it is necessary to protect them. It is important for
young children to realize that many resources are finite, and that we need
to reduce the amount of non-renewable energy that we use. Habits start at
an early age, and learning to turn off the water while brushing one's teeth
or to turn off the lights when they are not needed can easily become stan-
dard behavior.

Older children and teens are able to digest more scientific information
and appreciate how energy is harnessed. The books in this chapter use diagrams and charts to provide a clearer understanding. Photovoltaic cells and
windmills are just two of the many fascinating environmental tools we have,
and introducing these to young people helps them appreciate their value
and understand basic concepts and applications. The controversies surrounding such resources as fossil fuels and nuclear power also make interesting topics, especially for teens. There are many sides to these debates, and
books that address different viewpoints offer readers a more comprehensive
understanding of the issues.

The materials in this chapter help readers identify natural and other
energy resources and explain how those resources are used and/or misused.
Illustrations and diagrams accompany photographs and descriptive text to

supply the information in a way that is both comprehensive and interesting. The ability to harness resources such as wind and solar energy is as amazing as it can be overwhelming. When explained correctly, the science inspires both respect and hope for the future of Earth's resources.

FICTION

178 Bang, Molly. *My Light.*
GRADES: PS–2
Ill. by the author. Blue Sky Press, 2004, ISBN 978-0-439-48961-4, 33p. $16.95.
SUBJECTS: Solar energy—Fiction; Electricity—Fiction

This picture book is told from the point of view of the sun as it takes the reader on a journey exploring energy in its various forms. Bang uses this journey to explain how electricity ends up in our homes and introduces readers to the concepts of solar, wind, and water energy through non-threatening illustrations and detailed, accurate diagrams. There are four pages of supplemental energy facts at the end of the book. 🌍 🌳

Green, Jen.
SERIES: WHY SHOULD I? Barron's Educational

179 *Why Should I Save Energy?*
GRADES: PS–2
Ill. by Mike Gordon. 2005, pap., ISBN 978-0-7641-3156-1, 32p. $6.99.
SUBJECTS: Energy conservation—Fiction

180 *Why Should I Save Water?*
GRADES: PS–2
Ill. by Mike Gordon. 2005, pap., ISBN 978-0-7641-3157-8, 32p. $6.99.
SUBJECTS: Water conservation—Fiction

These informative fictional books are perfect for young readers. They deliver their information in a story that children can easily relate to, and each book is illustrated with multicultural cartoon characters. The text is large and describes environmental actions—of which there are many—throughout the books. A great choice for independent readers, these books are also helpful for parents and teachers, with tips for reading with children and follow-up activities. This series is highly recommended and should remain a timely resource for initiating conversations with children about environmental issues. ♻ ✪ ♣

WATCHING AND LISTENING GREEN

Banana Slug String Band.
Slug Music (BMI)

181 *Singing in Our Garden.*
GRADES: PS–6
CD. 2002, $15.00.
SUBJECTS: Ecology—Songs and music; Songs and music

182 *We All Live Downstream.*
GRADES: PS–6
CD. 2008, $15.00. 45 minutes
SUBJECTS: Ecology—Songs and music; Songs and music

This entertaining and educational band delivers toe-tapping, funny, and poignant music that lives up to the band's fun name. Being "slugs," these guys are concerned with Earth's natural resources, and their CDs include songs that teach children why it is important to respect the air, soil, and water. The *Singing in Our Garden* CD features songs that help explain the science of nature. "The Water Cycle Boogie, Air Cycle," and "Ecology" are three songs that urge children to protect the environment. The Banana Slug String Band takes a pointed look at the water cycle and water conservation in *We All Live Downstream*. With their call-and-response lyrics, high-quality production, robust instrumentals, and energetic, clear vocals, these CDs will have children (and adults, too!) singing and dancing. Includes a booklet with lyrics. ♻ ✪ ♣

183 Forest, Candy, and Nancy Schimmel. *Sun, Sun Shine: Songs for Curious Children.*
GRADES: PS–6
CD. Candy Forest and Nancy Schimmel, 2003, $15.00.

SUBJECTS: Environmental protection—Songs and music; Songs and music

All of the songs included on this CD explore historical and natural subjects, some of them addressing environmental topics as well. Using a combination of interesting musical instruments, infectious beats, and vocals provided by professional singers and a chorus of children, the songs are lively and fun. The song "Cycles" addresses the importance of recycling; "Sun, Sun Shine" celebrates the sun's power; and "Home in the Sky" is a sweet, sad song that asks if there is a heavenly habitat for endangered species. ♣

Lewis, Christopher, and Linda Lewis.
SERIES: ECO-KIDS EXPLORE. Landmark Media

184 *Ethanol.*
GRADES: 4–8
DVD. 2008, $195. 13 minutes
SUBJECTS: Alcohol as fuel

185 *Geothermal Energy.*
GRADES: 4–8
DVD. 2008, $195. 11 minutes
SUBJECTS: Geothermal energy

186 *Hybrid Cars.*
GRADES: 4–8
DVD. 2008, $195. 12 minutes
SUBJECTS: Hybrid electric cars

187 *Solar Power.*
GRADES: 4–8
DVD. 2008, $195. 17 minutes
SUBJECTS: Solar energy

188 *Wind Power.*
GRADES: 4–8
DVD. 2008, $195. 14 minutes
SUBJECTS: Wind power

The growing field of green power is the focus of this five-part series aimed at elementary and middle school audiences. Each video is approximately 15 minutes long and discusses one power source. Viewers learn about the history of the resource, its current use, and how it is harvested, gathered, or harnessed. Featuring diagrams, interviews, and step-by-step video clips, these programs are excellent resources that make a confusing subject less intimidating. ♻ ⊕

189 Suzuki, David, and Paula Salvador. *Build Green.*
GRADES: 8–12
DVD. Bullfrog Films, 2007, $250.
SUBJECTS: Sustainable architecture

This 45-minute film explores natural construction, energy independence, and the wise use of urban space. The construction portion of the film features homes built of rammed earth and straw and one house that captures the energy it needs from the sun. A section on urban and suburban growth discusses ideas to maximize and reuse urban spaces. Narrated and hosted by David Suzuki, this high-quality film is great for high school students, especially when paired with an assignment that asks students to design their own green buildings using the concepts they learn. ⊕

Tvedt, Terje, and Erik Hannemann.
SERIES: THE FUTURE OF WATER. Landmark Media

190 *The Future of Water: Part One: The Waterlords.*
GRADES: 10–12
DVD. 2008, $195. 52 minutes
SUBJECTS: Water supply; Water use

191 *The Future of Water: Part Two: The New Uncertainty.*
GRADES: 10–12
DVD. 2008, $195. 52 minutes
SUBJECTS: Water supply; Water use

192 *The Future of Water: Part Three: The Water Age.*
GRADES: 10–12
DVD. 2008, $195. 52 minutes
SUBJECTS: Water supply; Water use

In three hour-long films, Dr. Terje Tvedt travels to twenty-five countries to examine water use and the social, political, and health factors surrounding it. Part One uses dramatic footage of people struggling to obtain drinking water to emphasize the fact that this resource is in danger. Part Two explores the impact that rising sea levels will have on the Earth's landscape. Part Three is a look at conservation initiatives and other solutions, urging immediate action to protect this vital resource. ●

NONFICTION

Armentrout, David, and Patricia Armentrout.
SERIES: LET'S EXPLORE GLOBAL ENERGY. Rourke Publishing

193 *Biofuels.*
GRADES: 2–4
2008, ISBN 978-1-60472-321-2, 48p. $31.36.
SUBJECTS: Biomass energy

194 *Going Green.*
GRADES: 2–4
2008, ISBN 978-1-60472-323-6, 48p. $31.36.
SUBJECTS: Energy resources; Energy conservation

195 *Solar Energy.*
GRADES: 2–4
2009, ISBN 978-1-60472-325-0, 48p. $31.36.
SUBJECTS: Solar energy

196 *Wind Energy.*
GRADES: 2–4
2008, ISBN 978-1-60472-326-7, 48p. $31.36.
SUBJECTS: Wind power

The books in this series focus on alternative energy sources, how they can be used, and their future possibilities. The text is simple and easy to read, with highlighted vocabulary words and "Fuel for Thought" boxes with useful energy-saving tips. The bold, relevant photographs are emphasized by the books' colorful and playful design. Some books feature the advantages and disadvantages of alternative energy, and all books in the series include a glossary and an index. ✿ ●

Barnham, Kay.
SERIES: ENVIRONMENT ACTION! Crabtree Publishing

197 *Save Energy.*
GRADES: 1–3
2007, ISBN 978-0-7787-3660-8, 32p. $26.60.
SUBJECTS: Energy resources; Energy conservation

198 *Save Water.*
GRADES: 1–3
2008, ISBN 978-0-7787-3661-5, 32p. $26.60.
SUBJECTS: Water conservation

These books in the Environment Action! series explore energy and water conservation. Each book first examines the nature of the issue with large bright photographs, definitions, and fast facts. Then each book details steps that children can take to conserve natural resources. The large, simple text, glossaries, and indexes help beginning readers research conservation issues. ♲ 🌍

199 Binns, Tristan Boyer. *Bright Idea: Conserving Energy.*
GRADES: 3–5
SERIES: YOU CAN SAVE THE PLANET. Heinemann, 2005, ISBN 978-1-4034-6844-4, 32p. $19.75.
SUBJECTS: Energy conservation

Short, fact-filled paragraphs and bright contemporary pictures make this book easy to read. "Taking Action" boxes give the reader quick and easy ways to explore environmental activism and "Science Behind It" boxes offer readers a better understanding of nonrenewable energy. Case studies give real-life, hands-on examples of energy conservation, including "eco-schools." A bibliography encourages further research. ♲ 🌍

200 Bishop, Amanda. *Energy Conservation.*
GRADES: 2–4
SERIES: SAVING OUR WORLD. Marshall Cavendish, 2008, ISBN 978-0-7614-3224-1, 32p. $28.50.
SUBJECTS: Energy conservation; Environmentalism; Energy resources

Information about the importance of energy conservation and its impact on the environment, helpful environmental tips, and comprehension questions make this a valuable book. Large, dramatic photographs and an eye-catching design keep the material interesting and provide high-quality information about the subject. ✤ ◐

201 Bowden, Rob. *Earth's Water Crisis.*
GRADES: 5–7
SERIES: WHAT IF WE DO NOTHING? World Almanac Library, 2007, ISBN 978-0-8368-7754-0, 48p. $31.00.
SUBJECTS: Water conservation; Water quality

What if we do nothing to conserve the Earth's water supply? This book explores the health factors that should be considered and the legal battles that could arise concerning who owns the water supply. Theoretical questions ask the reader to consider water supply problems and their solutions. Answers are provided in the back of the book. ✤ ◐

202 Cartlidge, Cherese. *Alternative Energy.*
GRADES: 3–5
SERIES: RIPPED FROM THE HEADLINES: THE ENVIRONMENT. Erickson, 2008, ISBN 978-1-60217-022-3, 64p. $23.95.
SUBJECTS: Renewable energy resources

The issues surrounding alternative sources of energy are examined using charts, environmental vocabulary, photographs, and science concepts. The Ripped from the Headlines series uses a generous amount of well-documented quotations from a wide range of sources. ◐

Cooper, Sharon Katz.
SERIES: EXPLORING EARTH'S RESOURCES. Heinemann

203 *Learning from Fossils.*
GRADES: PS–2
2007, ISBN 978-1-4034-9317-0, 24p. $21.36.
SUBJECTS: Fossils; Natural resources

204 *Using Air.*
GRADES: PS–2
2007, ISBN 978-1-4034-9315-6, 24p. $21.36.
SUBJECTS: Air; Natural resources

205 *Using Coal, Oil, and Gas.*
GRADES: PS–2
2007, ISBN 978-1-4034-9318-7, 24p. $21.36.
SUBJECTS: Coal; Petroleum; Natural gas; Natural resources

206 *Using Plants.*
GRADES: PS–2
2007, ISBN 978-1-4034-9316-3, 24p. $21.36.
SUBJECTS: Plants; Natural resources

207 *Using Rocks.*
GRADES: PS–2
2007, ISBN 978-1-4034-9312-5, 24p. $21.36.
SUBJECTS: Rocks; Natural resources

208 *Using Soil.*
GRADES: PS–2
2007, ISBN 978-1-4034-9313-2, 24p. $21.36.
SUBJECTS: Soils; Natural resources

209 *Using Water.*
GRADES: PS–2
2007, ISBN 978-1-4034-9314-9, 24p. $21.36.
SUBJECTS: Water; Natural resources

This series for beginning readers provides information about Earth's natural resources. The simple text often describes the photographs that appear on each page. Each chapter begins with a question that helps readers comprehend the subject. An index, a glossary, and simple conservation tips are included in each book, and some include an easy-to-do experiment that complements the subject. ♻ ☺

....

210 Egendorf, Laura K., ed. *Energy Alternatives.*
GRADES: 7–10
SERIES: INTRODUCING ISSUES WITH OPPOSING VIEWPOINTS.
Greenhaven Press, 2006, ISBN 978-0-7377-3458-4, 120p. $33.70.
SUBJECTS: Energy resources; Renewable energy resources; Opposing viewpoints

The Introducing Issues with Opposing Viewpoints series targets a younger audience than the original Opposing Viewpoints series but uses the same format of contrasting articles, photographs, diagrams, quick facts, and comprehension questions. This book on energy alternatives covers energy consumption, the nature of energy alternatives, and the question of whether the world is suffering from an energy crisis. 🌐

---

211   Faust, Daniel R. *Energy Crisis: The Future of Fossil Fuels.*
GRADES: 3–6
SERIES: JR. GRAPHIC ENVIRONMENTAL DANGERS. PowerKids Press, 2009, ISBN 978-1-4042-4231-9, 24p. $23.95.
SUBJECTS: Energy resources; Fossil fuels

The energy crisis is illustrated in a dramatic story line that is based on fact. Equal parts entertainment and education, the Jr. Graphic Environmental Dangers series is good for reluctant readers and for children who need a nudge to get them started on their research. 🌐 🏆

---

212   Fisanick, Christina, ed. *Eco-Architecture.*
GRADES: 9–12
SERIES: OPPOSING VIEWPOINTS. Greenhaven Press, 2008, ISBN 978-0-7377-3996-1, 234p. $37.40.
SUBJECTS: Sustainable architecture; Opposing viewpoints

An introduction to the fairly new concept of eco-architecture. Brief, contrasting articles, comprehension questions, and resource lists will help students form their own opinions. Issues covered in this book include the benefits and drawbacks of eco-architecture, the question of whether urban sprawl is harmful to the environment, and the controversy about greenwashing. 🌐

Fridell, Ron.
SERIES: SAVING OUR LIVING EARTH. Lerner Publishing

213   *Earth-Friendly Energy.*
GRADES: 3–5
2009, ISBN 978-0-8225-7563-4, 71p. $30.60.
SUBJECTS: Renewable energy resources; Fossil fuels—Environmental aspects; Green movement

214   *Protecting Earth's Water Supply.*
GRADES: 3–5
2009, ISBN 978-0-8225-7557-3, 71p. $30.60.
SUBJECTS: Water pollution; Water conservation

From the Saving Our Living Earth series, these books look at alternative energies and water conservation. Real children and young adults working to improve the environment are featured. The detailed text, rich layouts, bold photographs, bibliography, index, and glossary are nice features that are included in all the books in the series. ✿ ❂

....

Friedman, Lauri S., ed.
SERIES: AN OPPOSING VIEWPOINTS GUIDE. Greenhaven Press

215 *Writing the Critical Essay: Energy Alternatives.*
GRADES: 7–12
2006, ISBN 978-0-7377-3200-9, 112p. $29.95.
SUBJECTS: Energy resources; Renewable energy resources; Opposing viewpoints; Opposing viewpoints

216 *Writing the Critical Essay: Oil.*
GRADES: 7–12
2008, ISBN 978-0-7377-4038-7, 128p. $29.95.
SUBJECTS: Petroleum products; Petroleum industry and trade; Opposing viewpoints; Opposing viewpoints

In the tradition of the Opposing Viewpoints series, the Opposing Viewpoints Guide series helps students evaluate and write critical essays. These books in the series cover topics relating to energy alternatives and the world's oil supply. The first section of each book presents brief, well-written articles representing contrasting opinions on the topics. The second and third sections provide writing examples and tools to prompt thoughtful evaluation and research, including model essays and facts for consideration. Wise choices for middle and high school collections. ❂

....

217 Friedman, Lauri S., and Jennifer Skancke, eds. *Oil.*
GRADES: 7–10
SERIES: INTRODUCING ISSUES WITH OPPOSING VIEWPOINTS. 2008, ISBN 978-0-7377-4171-1, 160p. $33.70.
SUBJECTS: Petroleum; Petroleum industry and trade; Fuel switching; Opposing viewpoints

Presenting brief, well-edited articles and examining both sides of the issues surrounding the use of oil, this book helps readers develop critical-thinking and research skills without using overly complicated language. Including color photographs, occasional cartoons, an annotated bibliography, comprehension questions, and quick fact boxes, this book uses many of the same strategies as the Opposing Viewpoints series for older readers while presenting the information on a level younger readers can comprehend.

....

218 Ganeri, Anita, and Chris Oxlade. *Down the Drain: Conserving Water.*
GRADES: 3–5
SERIES: YOU CAN SAVE THE PLANET. Heinemann, 2005, ISBN 978-1-4034-6851-2, 32p. $19.75.
SUBJECTS: Water conservation

Young readers will want to help conserve water after reading this book, which features "Taking Action" boxes that address why we need water, how water gets to our homes and schools, and wastewater. All books in the You Can Save the Planet series are excellent resources for young readers who want to understand environmental concerns such as water conservation.

....

219 Gifford, Clive. *Energy.*
GRADES: 6–8
SERIES: PLANET UNDER PRESSURE. Heinemann, 2006, ISBN 978-1-4034-7744-6, 48p. $22.
SUBJECTS: Energy resources

Gifford examines energy resources and how they are used in this book in the Planet Under Pressure series. Like the other books in the series, *Energy* uses photographs, timely facts and figures, charts, and diagrams to thoroughly examine the topic, and includes "What Do You Think?" and "What Can You Do?" boxes.

....

SERIES: ENERGY REVOLUTION. Crabtree Publishing

220 Gleason, Carrie. *Geothermal Energy: Using Earth's Furnace.*
GRADES: 3–6
2008, ISBN 978-0-7787-2917-4, 32p. $26.20.
SUBJECTS: Geothermal resources

221 Peppas, Lynne. *Ocean, Tidal, and Wave Energy: Power from the Sea.*
GRADES: 3–6

2008, ISBN 978-0-7787-2919-8, 32p. $26.20.
SUBJECTS: Tidal power; Ocean energy resources; Tidal power-plants

222 Walker, Niki. *Biomass: Fueling Change.*
GRADES: 3–6
2007, ISBN 978-0-7787-2914-3, 32p. $26.20.
SUBJECTS: Biomass energy

223 Walker, Niki. *Hydrogen: Running on Water.*
GRADES: 3–6
2007, ISBN 978-0-7787-2915-0, 32p. $26.20.
SUBJECTS: Hydrogen as fuel

Bright, colorful fonts and graphics make these books fun and easy to read. Case studies, conservation tips, and timelines make them high-quality informational resources—from their exciting, youthful covers to their indexes and glossaries. ♺ 🌐

Green, Jen.
SERIES: IMPROVING OUR ENVIRONMENT. Gareth Stevens Publishing

224 *Saving Energy.*
GRADES: 3–5
2005, ISBN 978-0-8368-4430-6, 32p. $19.50.
SUBJECTS: Energy conservation

225 *Saving Water.*
GRADES: 3–5
2005, ISBN 978-0-8368-4431-3, 32p. $19.50.
SUBJECTS: Water supply; Water conservation

Descriptive text combines with large photographs and bold design to make these books about energy and water conservation accessible to beginning readers. Fact boxes and experiments provide statistical information and hands-on experiences to engage the reader. Both books include a glossary, an index, and bibliographic information to aid in the reader's research. ♺ 🌐

Guillain, Charlotte.
SERIES: HELP THE ENVIRONMENT. Heinemann

226 *Saving Energy.*
GRADES: PS–2

2008, ISBN 978-1-4329-0887-4, 24p. $20.71.

SUBJECTS: Energy conservation

227 *Saving Water.*
GRADES: PS–2
2008, ISBN 978-1-4329-0886-7, 24p. $20.71.
SUBJECTS: Water conservation

By using simple words and repetitive phrases, these books help children rec-ognize ecological terms, become more environmentally conscious, and learn to read. The text is large and easy to read and is accompanied by photo-graphs of children conserving energy and water. Each book includes a glos-sary and an index to introduce young readers to research tools. ♻ 🌳

....

228 Gunkel, Darrin, ed. *Alternative Energy Sources.*
GRADES: 7–12
SERIES: CURRENT CONTROVERSIES. Greenhaven Press, 2006, ISBN 978-0-7377-3407-2, 204p. $37.40.
SUBJECTS: Renewable energy resources

The Current Controversies series uses brief, age-appropriate, and varied ar-ticles in comprehensive examinations of controversial subjects. In this vol-ume, articles address alternative energy issues including humans' reliance on fossil fuels, nuclear energy, and technologies such as biofuels and hybrid-electric energy. Each title in this series includes a list of organizations to con-tact, a bibliography, and an index. 🌐

....

229 Hall, Linley Erin, ed. *Critical Perspectives on Energy and Power.*
GRADES: 9–12
SERIES: SCIENTIFIC AMERICAN CRITICAL ANTHOLOGIES ON ENVIRONMENT AND CLIMATE. Rosen Publishing, 2006, ISBN 978-1-4042-0689-2, 206p. $31.95.
SUBJECTS: Energy resources

The books in this series consist of collections of *Scientific American* articles originally published between 1995 and 2005 that relate to energy and power resources. Most of the articles include black-and-white graphics such as di-agrams, charts, and illustrations to complement the text. High school stu-dents will find these useful for reports about energy use, future sources of energy, and the energy crisis. 🌐

230 Haugen, David M., ed. *Global Resources.*
GRADES: 9–12
SERIES: OPPOSING VIEWPOINTS. Greenhaven Press, 2008, ISBN 978-0-7377-3743-1, 233p. $37.40.
SUBJECTS: Natural resources; Opposing viewpoints

This book allows readers to develop their own opinions by presenting well-edited articles examining different views about the nature of global resources and whether or not they are in danger. Complementing the articles are occasional diagrams, charts, and even cartoons. Annotated bibliographies, comprehension questions, and fact boxes make this book an all-encompassing source on global resources. ☻

Hewitt, Sally.
SERIES: GREEN TEAM. Crabtree Publishing

231 *Using Energy.*
GRADES: 2–5
2009, ISBN 978-0-7787-4096-4, 32p. $26.60.
SUBJECTS: Energy resources

232 *Using Water.*
GRADES: 2–5
2009, ISBN 978-0-7787-4097-1, 32p. $26.60.
SUBJECTS: Water use

Lively yet focused layouts feature facts about using and conserving water and energy. Part of the new Green Team series, these books also feature step-by-step instructions for environmental activities that young children can accomplish. Diagrams and photographs help explain the importance of conserving natural resources. Up-to-date statistics and other information are delivered in age-appropriate language to ensure comprehension. ♺ ☻

233 Hirschmann, Kris. *Solar Energy.*
GRADES: 3–6
SERIES: OUR ENVIRONMENT. Kidhaven Press, 2005, ISBN 978-0-7377-3049-4, 48p. $26.20.
SUBJECTS: Solar energy

An exploration of solar energy, including how solar energy is harnessed and used. Children will come to understand a difficult concept through this well-designed, broad look at the issue. A glossary, an index, and a bibliography round out this entry in the Our Environment series. 🌐

Jakab, Cheryl.
SERIES: GLOBAL ISSUES. Smart Apple Media

234 *Energy Use.*
GRADES: 3–6
2007, ISBN 978-1-59920-126-9, 32p. $27.10.
SUBJECTS: Energy resources; Energy consumption

235 *Natural Resources.*
GRADES: 3–6
2008, ISBN 978-1-59920-125-2, 32p. $27.10.
SUBJECTS: Conservation of natural resources

The importance of using energy and other resources responsibly is introduced in these entries in the Global Issues series. Examples of uses of energy and of other natural resources help readers to understand the world around them and the impact of their everyday actions. Dynamic design adds interest to these valuable resources. 🌐

236 Jefferis, David. *Green Power: Eco-Energy Without Pollution.*
GRADES: 3–6
SERIES: SCIENCE FRONTIERS. Crabtree Publishing, 2006, ISBN 978-1-4177-8927-6, 32p. $19.95.
SUBJECTS: Renewable energy resources; Energy development

Using plenty of graphics and a nontraditional format, this entry in the Science Frontiers series packs in a ton of easy-to-understand scientific information about renewable energy sources such as hydroelectricity, ocean power, solar power, and wind turbines. Diagrams, photographs, and aerial images add interest. The last few chapters are dedicated to new and future green energy technologies. Also notable is the timeline of energy resource discoveries. 🌐

Juettner, Bonnie.
SERIES: OUR ENVIRONMENT. Kidhaven Press

237 *Energy.*
GRADES: 3–6

2004, ISBN 978-0-7377-1821-8, 48p. $26.20.
SUBJECTS: Energy resources; Energy industries

238 *Nuclear Power.*
GRADES: 3–6
2006, ISBN 978-0-7377-3618-2, 48p. $26.20.
SUBJECTS: Nuclear energy

In-depth, well-designed looks at energy and nuclear power, these resources provide readers with a well-rounded understanding of energy resources and the use of nuclear power as an alternative energy. Students will want to continue their research using the multimedia bibliographies in these books. ☻

239 Kallen, Stuart A. *World Energy Crisis.*
GRADES: 9–12
SERIES: COMPACT RESEARCH. ReferencePoint Press, 2008, ISBN 978-1-60152-011-1, 104p. $25.95.
SUBJECTS: Energy resources; Energy policy

Contrasting views of the world energy crisis are presented in this book in the Compact Research series. Statistics, primary source quotations, diagrams, and overviews give readers a broad look at the issue of world energy. Chapters cover the nature of fossil fuels, the debate about nuclear energy, and the possibilities of renewable energy sources. Information about key people and organizations involved in the world energy debate gives readers resources for further research. ☻

Knight, M. J.
SERIES: ONE SMALL STEP. Smart Apple Media

240 *Why Should I Switch Off the Light?*
GRADES: 2–4
2009, ISBN 978-1-59920-263-1, 32p. $27.10.
SUBJECTS: Energy conservation

241 Knight, M. J. *Why Should I Turn Off the Tap?*
GRADES: 2–4
2009, ISBN 978-1-59920-264-8, 32p. $27.10.
SUBJECTS: Water conservation

Readers will learn that even small actions can have big results in these two books in the One Small Step series. Every single spread includes "I Can Make a Difference" boxes with environmental tips and "One Small Fact" bubbles about conserving energy and water. These books include glossaries, Web sites, and indexes and are useful resources for impressing upon a young reader the importance of conservation. ♻ 🌎

....

SERIES: OPPOSING VIEWPOINTS. Greenhaven Press

242 Langwith, Jacqueline, ed. *Renewable Energy.*
GRADES: 9–12
2008, ISBN 978-0-7377-4226-8, 242p. $37.40.
SUBJECTS: Renewable energy resources; Opposing viewpoints

243 Logan, Michael, ed. *Coal.*
GRADES: 9–12
2007, ISBN 978-0-7377-3908-4, 256p. $37.40.
SUBJECTS: Coal; Energy resources; Opposing viewpoints

244 Nakaya, Andrea C., ed. *Oil.*
GRADES: 9–12
2006, ISBN 978-0-7377-3327-3, 244p. $37.40.
SUBJECTS: Petroleum industry and trade; Energy consumption; Opposing viewpoints

245 Passero, Barbara, ed. *Energy Alternatives.*
GRADES: 9–12
2006, ISBN 978-0-7377-3350-1, 238p. $37.40.
SUBJECTS: Renewable energy resources; Opposing viewpoints

Directed toward high school students, these books follow the Opposing Viewpoint format, using articles to present many different sides of the debates surrounding energy resources, renewable energy, and energy alternatives. The annotated bibliographies and comprehension questions provide further sources for research. 🌎

....

246 Lew, Kristi. *Goodbye Gasoline: The Science of Fuel Cells.*
GRADES: 5–7
SERIES: HEADLINE SCIENCE. Compass Point Books, 2009, ISBN 978-0-7565-3521-6, 48p. $20.99.
SUBJECTS: Fuel cells

Goodbye Gasoline uses dramatic layouts, contemporary photographs, historical fact boxes, and a timeline to relay information about how fuel cells convert chemicals to electricity, why fuel cells are considered "clean" energy, and what is left to be done in this field of science. Each chapter begins with a recent quote from recognizable news sources such as CBS and the *New York Times*. Includes bibliographic resources, a glossary, and source notes. ☻

247 McLeish, Ewan. *Sustainable Homes.*
GRADES: 2–4
SERIES: SUSTAINABLE FUTURES. Smart Apple Media, 2007, ISBN 978-1-58340-982-4, 48p. $31.35.
SUBJECTS: Eco-architecture

Energy-efficient homes and sustainable development are the focus of this book, which uses color photographs, charts, and case studies to explain the problems and solutions relating to environmental architecture and design. Questions and answers about sustainable architecture and planning will help readers understand the importance of this growing field. ♻ ☻

248 Morgan, Sally. *Conserving Our Fresh Water.*
GRADES: 2–4
SERIES: SUSTAINABLE FUTURES. Smart Apple Media, 2007, ISBN 978-1-58340-977-0, 48p. $31.35.
SUBJECTS: Water conservation; Fresh water

Using color photographs, relevant diagrams, and up-to-date statistical information, this book helps readers understand the world's reliance on a clean water supply and why it is important to conserve water and keep the supply clean. Case studies and question-and-answer sections add interest and make this book a good choice for reluctant readers. ♻ ☻

249 Morgan, Sally. *From Windmills to Hydrogen Fuel Cells: Discovering Alternative Energy.*
GRADES: 6–9
SERIES: CHAIN REACTIONS. Heinemann, 2007, ISBN 978-1-4034-9558-7, 64p. $24.00.
SUBJECTS: Renewable energy resources

This book examines the past, present, and future of conventional alternative energies such as wind, solar, and water power, as well as alternative energies such as nuclear, geothermal, biopower, and fuel cells. Complete with full-color diagrams, photographs, and fact boxes, this book looks at the culture and the science of alternative energy. Also included are a timeline, a glossary, and a section devoted to biographies of notable figures in alternative energy. ✪

....

Morris, Neil.
SERIES: GREEN KIDS. QEB

250 *Saving Energy.*
GRADES: K–3
2008, ISBN 978-1-5956-6541-6, 24p. $24.25.
SUBJECTS: Energy conservation

251 *Saving Water.*
GRADES: K–3
2008, ISBN 978-1-5956-6542-3, 24p. $24.25.
SUBJECTS: Water conservation

Playful layouts and a generous amount of photographs add life to these books in the Green Kids series. Peppered throughout the text are relevant statistics about conservation that are easy for this age range to understand (for example, "5 energy-saving light bulbs use the same amount of electricity as 1 ordinary light bulb"). Quirky illustrations feature kid-friendly characters and arrows pointing out important information, and there are "You Can Do It!" boxes. Includes an index. ♺ ✪ ♆

....

252 Nakaya, Andrea C. *Energy Alternatives.*
GRADES: 9–12
SERIES: COMPACT RESEARCH. ReferencePoint Press, 2008, ISBN 978-1-60152-017-3, 112p. $25.95.
SUBJECTS: Renewable energy resources

True to its name, the Compact Research series provides students comprehensive research tools on various subjects. This volume covers the subject of alternative energy through primary sources, diagrams, illustrations, statistics, and overviews. It also includes information about key people and organizations concerned with energy studies. ✪

ACTIVITIES FOR OLDER ENVIRONMENTALISTS

✳ Hands-On Experiment ✳

As a class, use a hands-on project to explain power resources. For example, create a wind-powered bubble machine as described in *Planet Earth: 25 Environmental Projects You Can Build Yourself* (see entry 270). This fun project is a great way to teach younger children about wind power.

Making a solar water heater as described in David Suzuki's *Eco-Fun: Great Projects, Experiments, and Games for a Greener Earth* will help students understand solar power. Give this experiment a southern twist by adding tea bags and creating "sun tea."

Consider a "green theme" for your annual science fair and encourage students to focus their projects on conservation or energy topics.

Field Trip Idea: Check whether there are any wind, water, or solar farms in your community and arrange a field trip to provide a firsthand look at how these natural resources are harvested and stored.

Nelson, Sara E.
SERIES: CARING FOR THE EARTH. Capstone Press

253 *Let's Save Energy!*
GRADES: PS–2
2007, ISBN 978-0-7368-6321-6, 24p. $12.95.
SUBJECTS: Energy conservation; Energy resources; Energy consumption

254 *Let's Save Water!*
GRADES: PS–2
2007, ISBN 978-0-7368-6322-3, 24p. $12.95.
SUBJECTS: Water conservation; Water pollution

These books in the Caring for the Earth series provide an introduction to the concepts of water and energy conservation with bright photographs, basic text, and vocabulary terms. The information and tips are both educational and environmentally useful, and the photographs depict young children doing their part to conserve natural resources. The glossary, index, and small bibliography help young readers with their beginning research skills. ♺ ⊕

---

255 Newton, David E. *Chemistry of the Environment.*
GRADES: 8–12
SERIES: THE NEW CHEMISTRY. Facts on File, 2007, ISBN 978-0-8160-5273-8, 228p. $35.00.
SUBJECTS: Environmental chemistry

An academic exploration of the role of chemistry in environmental issues such as pollution, waste disposal, and "green chemistry." Each topic is comprehensively discussed using statistics, research, diagrams, and articles. Also discussed are the social, cultural, and political implications of these issues. While it may not have broad appeal, this book is a valuable environmental science resource for older students. ⊕

---

256 Oxlade, Chris. *Energy Supplies.*
GRADES: 4–6
SERIES: ACTION FOR THE ENVIRONMENT. Smart Apple Media, 2006, ISBN 978-1-58340-597-0, 32p. $27.10.
SUBJECTS: Energy resources

A short but complete overview of the uses and limitations of energy resources and alternative energies. Large, easy-to-read text and bold, relevant photographs draw readers into the subject matter. Each chapter features "Action Stations" that give young readers ideas to conserve energy. ♺ ⊕

SERIES: FUELING THE FUTURE. Heinemann

257 Oxlade, Chris. *Solar Energy.*
GRADES: 3–6
2008, ISBN 978-1-4329-1564-3, 32p. $28.21.
SUBJECTS: Solar energy; Energy resources

258 Raum, Elizabeth. *Fossil Fuels and Biofuels.*
GRADES: 3–6
2008, ISBN 978-1-4329-1562-9, 32p. $28.21.
SUBJECTS: Fossil fuels; Energy resources; Biomass energy

259 Raum, Elizabeth. *Nuclear Energy.*
GRADES: 3–6
2008, ISBN 978-1-4329-1563-6, 32p. $28.21.
SUBJECTS: Nuclear energy; Energy resources

260 Raum, Elizabeth. *Water and Geothermal Energy.*
GRADES: 3–6
2008, ISBN 978-1-4329-1565-0, 32p. $28.21.
SUBJECTS: Geothermal energy; Energy resources

261 Raum, Elizabeth. *Wind Energy.*
GRADES: 3–6
2008, ISBN 978-1-4329-1572-8, 32p. $28.21.
SUBJECTS: Wind energy; Energy resources

A focused series of books about alternative energies. Each book in the series explores many facets of an energy source, including how energy is generated from it, why the energy is useful, complications of the energy source, and possibilities for its future. Each book includes maps, a timeline, descriptive photographs, glossaries, a list of affiliated organizations, an index, and a multimedia bibliography. 🌐

Parker, Russ.
SERIES: PLANET IN CRISIS. Rosen Publishing

262 *Energy Supplies in Crisis.*
GRADES: 3–6
2009, ISBN 978-1-4358-5251-8, 32p. $25.25.
SUBJECTS: Energy resources; Renewable energy resources; Energy conservation

263 *Water Supplies in Crisis.*
GRADES: 3–6
2009, ISBN 978-1-4358-5250-1, 32p. $25.25.
SUBJECTS: Water supply; Water use

Large in size and featuring two-page spreads, "hot topic" boxes, progression charts, and diagrams, these volumes in the Planet in Crisis series present quick but comprehensive looks at the Earth's energy and water supplies. Readers will enjoy the contemporary layouts that are busy and bright and the current and reliable information about humans' reliance on energy, alternative energy sources, and the status of the world's water supply. Each volume includes organizational contacts, a bibliography, an index, and a glossary. ♻ 🌐

Petersen, Christine.
SERIES: A TRUE BOOK—ENVIRONMENT AND CONSERVATION.
Children's Press

264　*Alternative Energy.*
GRADES: PS–2
2004, ISBN 978-0-516-22804-4, 48p. $25.00.
SUBJECTS: Renewable energy resources

265　*Solar Power.*
GRADES: PS–2
2004, ISBN 978-0-516-22807-5, 48p. $25.00.
SUBJECTS: Solar energy

266　*Water Power.*
GRADES: PS–2
2004, ISBN 978-0-516-22808-2, 48p. $25.00.
SUBJECTS: Water power

267　*Wind Power.*
GRADES: PS–2
2004, ISBN 978-0-516-22809-9, 48p. $25.00.
SUBJECTS: Wind power

These books for beginning readers explore the use of energy from water, the wind, and the sun. Excellent introductions to the scientific and social aspects of the environment and conservation, the books in this series feature multimedia bibliographies, glossaries, and indexes. ♲ ⊛

Povey, Karen D.
SERIES: OUR ENVIRONMENT. Kidhaven Press

268　*Biofuels.*
GRADES: 3–6
2006, ISBN 978-0-7377-3560-4, 48p. $26.20.
SUBJECTS: Biomass energy

269　*Hybrid Cars.*
GRADES: 3–6
2006, ISBN 978-0-7377-3484-3, 48p. $26.20.
SUBJECTS: Hybrid electric cars; Automobiles

Colorful diagrams, photographs, and accessible vocabulary help explain bio-fuels and hybrid cars in these books in the Our Environment series. Students will discover how these new energies and their effects on the environment are different from other energy sources. *Biofuels* and *Hybrid Cars* will appeal to students because of their subject matter and to adults because of their accuracy and relevance. 🌐

270 Reilly, Kathleen. *Planet Earth: 25 Environmental Projects You Can Build Yourself.*
GRADES: 3–6
SERIES: BUILD IT YOURSELF. Nomad Press, 2008, pap., ISBN 978-1-934670-04-0, 128p. $14.95.
SUBJECTS: Environmental education; Environmental protection

With more than twenty interactive projects, tons of tips, and scientific information, this book is an invaluable resource for environmental education. Children can learn about renewable energy sources while making a wind-powered bubble machine and about responsible waste disposal by making a worm composting castle. With detailed instructions, graphics, and supplemental environmental and scientific information, this is a must-have for science teachers and parents with curious children. ♻ 🌐 🌳

Royston, Angela.
SERIES: ECO-ACTION. Heinemann

271 *Buildings of the Future: Eco-Action.*
GRADES: 6–8
2008, ISBN 978-1-4329-0126-4, 48p. $22.00.
SUBJECTS: Sustainable buildings; Carbon dioxide mitigation; Global warming; Eco-architecture

272 *Consumerism of the Future: Eco-Action.*
GRADES: 6–8
2008, ISBN 978-1-4329-0128-8, 48p. $22.00.
SUBJECTS: Consumption; Consumer behavior; Global warming

273 *Energy of the Future: Eco-Action.*
GRADES: 6–8
2008, ISBN 978-0-431-02989-4, 48p. $22.00.
SUBJECTS: Renewable energy resources

274 *Travel of the Future: Eco-Action.*
GRADES: 6–8
2008, ISBN 978-1-4329-0127-1, 48p. $22.00.
SUBJECTS: Transportation engineering; Ecotourism; Carbon dioxide mitigation; Global warming

Focusing on developing technologies and initiatives to prevent the effects of global warming, this series balances a realistic look at the issues with a positive glimpse into the future. The science is accessible and cool—perfect for middle school readers. Each book in the series comes equipped with an index and a glossary as well as an extensive Web site list. ♲ ✪

---

275 Rybolt, Thomas R., and Robert C. Mebane. *Environmental Science Fair Projects Using Water, Feathers, Sunlight, Balloons, and More.*
GRADES: 4–6
SERIES: EARTH SCIENCE! BEST SCIENCE PROJECTS. Ill. by Tom LaBaff.
Enslow Publishers, 2005, ISBN 978-0-7660-2364-2, 128p. $26.60.
SUBJECTS: Environmental science; Science projects

With more than 20 environmental science experiments, this book is an excellent source for science students and teachers. The five chapters focus on air, water, soil, pollution, and energy, and all begin with an introduction before delving into the experiments. Each experiment provides a list of materials, detailed steps, and further ideas for science fair projects. This book is made even more helpful by black-and-white illustrations, a bibliography, and an index. ♲ ✪

---

276 Sawvel, Patty Jo, ed. *Water Resource Management.*
GRADES: 7–10
SERIES: INTRODUCING ISSUES WITH OPPOSING VIEWPOINTS.
Greenhaven Press, 2008, ISBN 978-0-7377-3979-4, 158p. $33.70.
SUBJECTS: Water resources management; Water—Law and legislation; Water quality management; Opposing viewpoints

Short articles examining many issues involving water resource management help readers to develop critical thinking skills. Topics covered in this book include the relationship between global warming and water resources; conserving wetlands; and regulation of water supplies. This series serves a younger audience than the Opposing Viewpoints series but includes many of the trusted features of the series for older readers, including color photographs, occasional cartoons, annotated bibliographies, comprehension questions, and quick fact boxes. ✪

277 Sherman, Jill. *Oil and Energy Alternatives.*
GRADES: 7–10
SERIES: ESSENTIAL VIEWPOINTS. Abdo Publishing, 2008, ISBN 978-1-60453-110-7, 112p. $32.79.
SUBJECTS: Petroleum industry and trade; Renewable energy resources

The statistical, biographical, and legislative information included in this book is helpful to student researchers. *Oil and Energy Alternatives* and the other books in the Essential Viewpoints series take a balanced approach to discussing sometimes controversial issues. By using anecdotes, text boxes, a timeline, and other research features, this book gives students a broad look at a complicated subject. ♻ 🌐

Snedden, Robert.
SERIES: ESSENTIAL ENERGY. Heinemann

278 *Energy Alternatives.*
GRADES: 3–6
2007, pap., ISBN 978-0-431-11810-9, 48p. $19.95.
SUBJECTS: Renewable energy resources; Energy resources

279 *Energy from Fossil Fuels.*
GRADES: 3–6
2006, ISBN 978-1-57572-442-3, 48p. $31.43.
SUBJECTS: Fossil fuels; Energy resources

280 *Energy Transfer.*
GRADES: 3–6
2006, ISBN 978-1-4034-8733-9, 48p. $19.95.
SUBJECTS: Energy transfer

281 *Nuclear Energy.*
GRADES: 3–6
2006, ISBN 978-1-4034-8734-6, 48p. $19.95.
SUBJECTS: Nuclear energy; Nuclear power plants

Packed with information, fast facts, historical illustrations, and current photographs, the books in this series explore why and how energy resources are obtained, explaining the dangers and the environmental impacts of each resource. Each book includes a glossary. 🌐

282 Spilsbury, Louise. *Running Water: Our Most Precious Resource.*
GRADES: 3–6
SERIES: GEOGRAPHY FOCUS. Raintree Publishers, 2006, ISBN 978-1-4109-1116-2, 48p. $31.43.
SUBJECTS: Water

The nature of water as a natural resource and the importance of water conservation are conveyed to readers in short, information-packed paragraphs and fast fact boxes. This book, like the other titles in the Geography Focus series, is attractive, dynamic, and contemporary. ✪

283 Spilsbury, Louise, and Richard Spilsbury. *Water.*
GRADES: 6–8
SERIES: PLANET UNDER PRESSURE. Heinemann, 2007, ISBN 978-1-4034-8214-3, 48p. $22.00.
SUBJECTS: Water—Environmental aspects; Water conservation; Hydrologic cycle; Water use

How are water resources used? What can we do to conserve water? Photographs, timely facts and figures, charts, and diagrams help to answer readers' questions about water. Readers will be challenged to think for themselves by the "What Do You Think?" and "What Can You Do?" features in this book. ♲ ✪

284 Spilsbury, Richard, and Louise Spilsbury. *The Earth's Resources.*
GRADES: 4–6
SERIES: SCIENCE ON FILE. Chelsea House, 2006, ISBN 978-0-7910-8863-0, 47p. $20.25.
SUBJECTS: Natural resources; Conservation of natural resources; Environmental protection

Featuring a colorful design accentuated by bright photographs and descriptive illustrations, this is an excellent source of quick information about natural resources. Fossil fuels, polymers, water, air, and even crystal resources are included. Focus boxes, historical information, and activities add to this book's usefulness. ✪

285 Stille, Darlene R. *Natural Resources: Using and Protecting Earth's Supplies.*
GRADES: 5–7
SERIES: EXPLORING SCIENCE. Compass Point Books, 2005, ISBN 978-0-7565-0856-2, 48p. $20.95.
SUBJECTS: Natural resources; Energy resources

The emphasis of this book is more on content than on design. Alhough it includes fact boxes and design elements that break up the text, it has a more sophisticated tone than do many books for this age group. Subtle fonts and graphics explain the importance of protecting natural resources, and the author's deep knowledge of the subject is evident. For the serious researcher. ◐

286 Stoyles, Pennie, and Peter Pentland. *Nuclear Energy.*
GRADES: 2–4
SERIES: SCIENCE ISSUES. Smart Apple Media, 2003, ISBN 978-1-58340-331-0, 32p. $27.10.
SUBJECTS: Nuclear energy

This book in the Science Issues series helps students navigate the confusing topic of nuclear energy using in-depth text, diagrams, and charts. The authors of *Nuclear Energy* are careful to present many different sides of the nuclear energy debate and to include a generous number of comprehension questions. ◐

287 Strauss, Rochelle. *One Well: The Story of Water on Earth.*
GRADES: 3–5
SERIES: KIDS CAN MAKE A DIFFERENCE. Ill. by Rosemary Woods. Kids Can Press, 2007, ISBN 978-1-55337-954-6, 32p. $17.95.
SUBJECTS: Water; Water conservation

The water cycle is carefully explained in this colorful and unique picture book. Facts about the nature of water supplement the text. Woods's delicate and detailed illustrations are rich with blues and greens to complement the story. Charts, tables, an index, and conservation information add to this book's appeal to both children and educators. ♳ ◐ ♉

288 Stringer, John. *Energy.*
GRADES: 2–4
SERIES: SUSTAINABLE FUTURES. Smart Apple Media, 2007, ISBN 978-1-58340-979-4, 48p. $31.35.
SUBJECTS: Energy resources

Intriguing headings invite readers to explore the issues surrounding energy resources in this book in the Sustainable Futures series. Energy conservation is the focus, and the topics discussed include fossil fuels, renewable energy sources, biofuels, and energy efficiency. The last chapter includes tips for young readers interested in energy conservation in their homes and schools. A glossary, multimedia bibliography, and index are also included. ♻ 🌍

Tabak, John.
SERIES: ENERGY AND THE ENVIRONMENT. Facts on File

289 *Biofuels.*
GRADES: 9–12
2009, ISBN 978-0-8160-7082-4, 204p. $40.00.
SUBJECTS: Biofuels; Biomass energy

290 *Coal and Oil.*
GRADES: 9–12
2009, ISBN 978-0-8160-7083-1, 208p. $40.00.
SUBJECTS: Coal; Petroleum products; Fossil fuels

291 *Natural Gas and Hydrogen.*
GRADES: 9–12
2009, ISBN 978-0-8160-7084-8, 224p. $40.00.
SUBJECTS: Natural gas; Gas as fuel; Hydrogen

292 *Nuclear Energy.*
GRADES: 9–12
2009, ISBN 978-0-8160-7085-5, 224p. $40.00.
SUBJECTS: Nuclear energy

293 *Solar and Geothermal Energy.*
GRADES: 9–12
2009, ISBN 978-0-8160-7086-2, 224p. $40.00.

SUBJECTS: Solar energy; Geothermal energy; Renewable energy resources

294 *Wind and Water.*
GRADES: 9–12
2009, ISBN 978-0-8160-7087-9, 224p. $40.00.
SUBJECTS: Wind energy; Water energy; Renewable energy resources

In this six-volume series devoted to the topic of energy production, Tabak explores the history, science, and legislation relating to natural and alternative energies. Each volume presents a comprehensive look at an energy source, including its limitations and any controversies that surround it. A great resource for this age range, this series balances information with comprehension and includes interviews of prominent people in the field. ☻

295 Welsbacher, Anne. *Earth-Friendly Design.*
GRADES: 3–5
SERIES: SAVING OUR LIVING EARTH. Lerner Publishing, 2009, ISBN 978-0-8225-7564-1, 71p. $30.60.
SUBJECTS: Design—Environmental aspects; Green technology; Eco-architecture

This book presents a comprehensive look at the subject of designing houses and other buildings with the environment in mind. Text boxes with interesting facts help to draw readers into the material. Another excellent book in the Saving Our Living Earth series, this volume includes detailed scientific facts, a vibrant layout, an index, a bibliography, and a glossary. ♲ ☻

296 Welton, Jude. *Water Supplies.*
GRADES: 4–6
SERIES: ACTION FOR THE ENVIRONMENT. Smart Apple Media, 2006, ISBN 978-1-58340-601-4, 32p. $27.10.
SUBJECTS: Water supply

Large, bold text and colorful pictures enliven the content of this title in the Action for the Environment series. Brief chapters explain the importance of conserving and cleaning the world's water supply. Students will be inspired by the "Action Stations" in every chapter that provide examples of responsible and clever ways to improve the environment. ♲ ☻

Wheeler, Jill C.
SERIES: EYE ON ENERGY. Abdo Publishing

297 *Alternative Cars.*
GRADES: 2–4
2007, ISBN 978-1-59928-803-1, 32p. $24.21.
SUBJECTS: Alternative fuel vehicles

298 *Fossil Fuels.*
GRADES: 2–4
2007, ISBN 978-1-59928-805-5, 32p. $24.21.
SUBJECTS: Fossil fuels

299 *Nature Power.*
GRADES: 2–4
2007, ISBN 978-1-59928-806-2, 32p. $24.21.
SUBJECTS: Renewable energy resources

300 *Nuclear Power.*
GRADES: 2–4
2007, ISBN 978-1-59928-807-9, 32p. $24.21.
SUBJECTS: Nuclear energy

301 *Renewable Fuels.*
GRADES: 2–4
2007, ISBN 978-1-59928-808-6, 32p. $24.21.
SUBJECTS: Renewable energy resources

This new series provides lots of useful conservation tips. Its dynamic design features bright photographs and engages readers with "Fact or Fiction" boxes and "Energy Buzz" boxes. Full of relevant information delivered in a stylish layout, these books are a very smart purchase for the children's nonfiction collection. ♻ ⊕

302 Winters, Adam. *Destruction of Earth's Resources: The Need for Sustainable Development.*
GRADES: 7–12
SERIES: EXTREME ENVIRONMENTAL THREATS. Rosen Publishing, 2007, ISBN 978-1-4042-0746-2, 64p. $29.25.
SUBJECTS: Sustainable development; Economic development—Environmental aspects; Environmental policy

This book in the Extreme Environmental Threats series examines the harmful destruction of natural resources and the importance of protecting the Earth's ecosystems. Although it is aimed at students in grades 7–12, the book's layout and length will appeal to younger audiences or to older students with lower reading skills. Tables, fast facts, color photographs, an extensive bibliography, a glossary, and an index make this a valuable research tool. 🌐

---

303 Woodford, Chris. *Energy.*
GRADES: 3–6
SERIES: SEE FOR YOURSELF. DK Publishing, 2007, ISBN 978-0-7566-2561-0, 64p. $14.99.
SUBJECTS: Energy resources

Do not be fooled by the fact that this book in the See for Yourself series looks like a picture book—it packs a scientific punch. Unique layouts, colorful photography, and informative captions help the reader to fully understand the subject of energy. Younger readers will be drawn in by the design of the book and older readers will respect the large amount of information in its pages. 🌐

RECYCLED FAVORITES

304 Gardner, Robert. *Science Projects About the Environment and Ecology.*
GRADES: 6–9
SERIES: SCIENCE PROJECTS. Enslow Publishers, 1999, ISBN 978-0-89490-951-1, 112p. $26.60.
SUBJECTS: Environmental science; Ecology—Experiments; Science projects

More than twenty-five science fair-worthy experiments on subjects such as decomposition, the greenhouse effect, recycling, pollution, and alternative energy will give students new perspectives on the material. Black-and-white drawings, graphs, and tables provide clarification. Background information is useful, but general enough that this book will not be soon outdated. The experiments are straightforward and the safety warnings are clear, making this book both smart and safe. ♻ 🌐

EARTH'S RESOURCES STORYTIME

Begin with "Good Morning, Dear Earth."

> *Good morning, dear Earth*
> *Good morning, dear Sun (hold your hands above your head)*
> *Good morning, dear stones (put a "stone" in your hand)*
> *And the flowers, every one. (make your hand into a flower)*
>
> *Good morning, dear bees (fly a "bee" around between your fingers)*
> *And the birds in the trees (make your arms into wings and flap them)*
> *Good morning to you (point to the children)*
> *And good morning to me. (point to yourself)*

> *"Good morning, children. Today we're going to discuss something called 'natural resources.' Natural resources are all around us—dirt, trees, water, wind, and even the sun. We all need and use these resources. Let's start with a story."*

Read *Uno's Garden* by Graeme Base (see entry 84).

> *"Have you ever seen a snortlepig before? Maybe not, but I bet you have seen trees and flowers! Trees and flowers need clean earth, air, and rain to grow. I know a song about flowers. Let's start off as little seeds."*

Squat down and curl up into a ball and encourage the children to do so.

Sing "Little Flower" (to the tune of "Pop Goes the Weasel").

> *Little flower in the ground*
> *Sitting oh-so-still.*
> *Little flower, will you sprout?*
> *Yay! Yes I will! (on "Yay!" Jump up and stretch out your arms)*
> *(repeat a couple of times)*

> *"The sun helps flowers grow and does many other amazing things. We can even use special equipment to get energy from the sun. Energy is what makes you play and dance, but we need a different kind of energy to turn on the lights or watch TV. Did you know that scientists can get energy from the wind? What else can the wind do? It can make your kite fly high!"*

Play the kite game. (Before storytime, make seven kites of appropriate colors with white on one side of the kite. As you say the rhymes fly the white side of the kite and allow the children time to guess the color, then reveal the color to them.)

I saw a kite fly overhead. Guess what color it was. It was red.
I saw a kite fall below. Guess what color it was. It was yellow.
I saw a kite stuck in a tree. Guess what color it was. It was green.
I saw a kite fly out of sight. Guess what color it was. It was white.
I saw a kite fly over you. Guess what color it was. It was blue.
I saw a kite fall down, down, down. Guess what color it was. It was brown.
I saw a kite so pretty it glowed. Guess what color it was. It was a rainbow!

"Scientists are able to take the wind that lifts kites into the sky and make electricity with it! That's pretty cool, but it is needed because we are using too much of our other sources of energy, like the gasoline that goes into cars. It is important that we save energy so there is plenty to go around for many, many years."

Read *Let's Save Energy!* by Sara E. Nelson (see entry 253).

"We learned a lot of valuable lessons from that book. What are some of the things we should do to save energy? I know a song that will help us remember."

Sing "Help Save the Earth" (to the tune of "Here We Go 'Round the Mulberry Bush").

This is the way we walk to the store (walk in place)
Walk to the store, walk to the store
This is the way we walk to the store
To help save the Earth.

Second verse: This is the way we turn off the lights (put your arms in
          the air and bring them down to cover your eyes)
Third verse: This is the way we take the bus (sit down and stand up)

"I hope we all remember to walk, ride our bikes, or take the bus when we can, and turn off the lights and TV when we aren't using them. If we all do that we can help fight global warming and save the ice caps. I know I will!"

Sing "If You Love Earth and You Know It" (to the tune of "If You're Happy and You Know It").

If you love Earth and you know it, clap your hands!
If you love Earth and you know it, clap your hands!
If you love Earth and you know it, then let your actions show it!
If you love Earth and you know it, clap your hands!

Second verse: If you love Earth and you know it, stomp your feet!

Third verse: If you love Earth and you know it, shout "Reduce!"
If you love Earth and you know it, shout "Reuse!"
If you love Earth and you know it, then let your actions show it!
If you love Earth and you know it, shout "Recycle!"

RECYCLING

RECYCLING IS SIMPLE. THE ACTUAL PROCESSES THAT materials go through to be recycled are not simple by any means, but the steps humans take to recycle are easy. What takes more effort is making recycling accessible. Until everyone is in the habit of recycling, though, it will not be accessible to all. The best way to create good habits is to start early and that is where all of the books in this chapter help.

The books for the youngest readers cultivate good habits by showing identifiable characters recycling and reusing materials. Often these books explain that all garbage has to go somewhere and that is why it is important to reduce waste. Discussions about landfills and recyclable material can begin early: What child doesn't want to talk about trash? Creative ideas for reusing material can even make recycling fun.

Books for older children and teens have the ability to motivate. Many books encourage readers not only to recycle but also to start recycling programs in their schools or communities. Readers will be inspired by the numerous ideas for turning old items into masterpieces and other trendy "green" art projects that use recycled materials. Descriptive diagrams and photographs that explain the recycling process in detail will captivate readers interested in science.

The books in this chapter help readers learn how and why to recycle as well as what happens when materials are recycled. To varying degrees, these titles educate, reiterate, and inspire children and teens to examine their homes, schools, and communities to make recycling a habit and accessible to all. Recycling can be very, very easy.

....

FICTION

305 Bethel, Ellie. *Michael Recycle.*
GRADES: PS–2
Ill. by Alexandra Colombo. Worthwhile Books, 2008, ISBN 978-1-60010-224-0, 28p. $15.99.
SUBJECTS: Recycling—Fiction

This fun picture book glamorizes recycling while at the same time showing young readers that it is easy to do. Told in playful rhyming verse, it is the story of a caped crusader who teaches the town of Abberdoo-Rimey the importance of recycling. Colorful, detailed illustrations give an effect similar to animation. This book begs to be read aloud and will be requested again and again. ♻ 🌳

....

306 Green, Jen. *Why Should I Recycle?*
GRADES: PS–2
SERIES: WHY SHOULD I? Ill. by Mike Gordon. Barron's Educational, 2005, pap., ISBN 978-0-7641-3155-4, 32p. $6.99.
SUBJECTS: Recycling—Fiction; Refuse and refuse disposal—Fiction

Perfect for young readers, this book delivers information in a story that kids can easily identify with, illustrated with multicultural cartoon characters. The text is large and describes the environmental actions—of which there are many—that appear throughout the book. A great choice for independent readers, this book is also helpful for parents and teachers, with tips for reading this book with children and follow-up activities. This series is highly recommended and should remain a timely resource for initiating conversations with children about environmental issues. ♻ 🌍 🌳

....

Inches, Alison.
SERIES: LITTLE GREEN BOOKS. Little Simon

307 *The Adventures of a Plastic Bottle: A Story About Recycling.*
GRADES: PS–2
Ill. by Pete Whitehead. 2009, pap., ISBN 978-1-4169-6788-0, 24p. $3.99.
SUBJECTS: Recycling—Fiction; Environmental Protection—Fiction

308 *I Can Save the Earth! One Little Monster Learns to Reduce, Reuse, and Recycle.*
GRADES: PS–2
Ill. by Viviana Garofoli. 2008, pap., ISBN 978-1-4169-6789-7, 24p. $3.99.
SUBJECTS: Recycling—Fiction; Environmental Protection—Fiction

Two of the first **volumes** in Simon & Schuster's new Little Green series, these books introduce young readers to the concepts of reducing, reusing, and recycling by using playful, fictional narratives. The bright, cartoon illustrations are lively and the stories are interesting enough to hold young readers' attention and reinforce good environmental habits. The Adventures of a Plastic Bottle follows the path of a plastic bottle in an informative, but light-hearted tale of the importance of recycling. 🔄 🌳

309 McDonald, Megan. *Judy Moody Saves the World.*
GRADES: 2–4
SERIES: JUDY MOODY. Ill. by Peter H. Reynolds. Walker Books Ltd., 2006, pap., ISBN 978-1-4063-0212-7, 160p. $5.99.
SUBJECTS: Environmental protection—Fiction; Recycling—Fiction

This third installment in the Judy Moody series features the high-spirited third-grader trying to save the world one rubber toilet plunger at a time. The cute, black-and-white cartoon illustrations help tell the story of how Judy starts a class recycling project. The quirky characters and witty text will keep readers delighted and they will probably pick up some environmental ideas of their own. 🔄 🌳

310 Taback, Simms. *Joseph Had a Little Overcoat.*
GRADES: PS–2
Ill. by the author. Viking, 1999, ISBN 978-0-670-87855-0, 32p. $16.99.
SUBJECTS: Folklore—Fiction; Recycling—Fiction

Winner of the 2000 Caldecott Medal and originally a story of thrift, this classic story is a perfect example of reusing. Joseph's coat is old and worn and as it frays he makes new garments from the remains—a jacket, a vest, and so forth—until he ends up with a button. Colorful illustrations have a playful element and peek-a-boo cutouts allow the reader to guess what clothing item is coming next. 🌳

311 Tafolla, Carmen. *Baby Coyote and the Old Woman / El Coyotito y la viejita: A Bilingual Celebration of Friendship and Ecological Wisdom / Una celebracion bilingue de la amistad y la sabiduria ecologica.*
GRADES: K–3
Ill. by Matt Novak. Wings Press, 2000, ISBN 978-0-930324-48-3, 24p. $17.95.
SUBJECTS: Recycling—Fiction; Coyote—Fiction; Spanish language—Fiction

The subtitle of this cute bilingual picture book should be: *A Modern Ecological Folk Tale.* Baby Coyote and the old woman have a friendly, if passive relationship until the old woman begins to accumulate garbage behind her desert home. Baby Coyote moves the old woman's trash to her front doorstep to show her how important it is to reduce and reuse her waste and recycle when she can. The illustrations are bright, sweet, and expressive and each page features both English and Spanish text. 🌳

312 Wallace, Nancy Elizabeth. *Recycle Every Day!*
GRADES: K–2
Ill. by the author. Marshall Cavendish, 2006, ISBN 978-0-7614-5149-5, 32p. $16.95.
SUBJECTS: Recycling—Fiction; Refuse and refuse disposal—Fiction; Rabbits—Fiction

Nancy Wallace's recognizable and loved character Minna explores the many different ways in which she and her rabbit family can recycle every day. Wallace's characteristic collage illustrations use recycled materials that are featured in the back of this picture book. At the back of the book there is a game/activity that presents a recycling calendar and is entertaining and informative. ♻ 🌳

313 Wong, Janet S. *The Dumpster Diver.*
GRADES: PS–2
Ill. by David Roberts. Candlewick Press, 2007, ISBN 978-0-7636-2380-7, 32p. $16.99.
SUBJECTS: Recycling—Fiction; Inventions—Fiction; Neighbors—Fiction

This cleverly illustrated picture book makes reusing garbage cool! A group of kids turn dumpster diving into an adventure, using their finds to create new and sometimes useful objects. The text is placed on the pages using a collage technique and David Roberts's illustrations are playful, unique, and multicultural. Without specifically mentioning recycling or the importance of reducing waste, this book will please young, creative minds that enjoy a sense of adventure. ♣

314 Yee, Wong Herbert. *A Brand-New Day with Mouse and Mole.*
GRADES: PS–2
SERIES: MOUSE AND MOLE. Ill. by the author. Houghton Mifflin, 2008, ISBN 978-0-618-96676-9, 48p. $15.00.
SUBJECTS: Recycling—Fiction; Clothing and dress—Fiction; Friendship—Fiction

This sweet tale about Mouse and Mole follows the good friends through an ordinary day. Complementing the beginning-reader text are simple, gentle illustrations that are also expressive. What makes this book an excellent choice for environmental collections is the subtle message in Mouse and Mole's actions. They each take something old and make it into something new for the benefit of the other. A good recommendation for fans of Frog and Toad. ♣

WATCHING AND LISTENING GREEN

315 Johnson, Jack, songwriter/singer. *"3 R's."*
GRADES: PS–2
CD, *Sing-A-Longs and Lullabies for the Film Curious George.*
Universal Records, 2006. 2:26 minutes
SUBJECTS: Recycling; Songs and music

"3 R's" is an upbeat and informative song that teaches children to reduce, reuse, and recycle. Jack Johnson's characteristic easy-going vocals partner with inspiring lyrics and even a little math skills thrown in to create a great song. MP3 versions of this song are available at various Internet sites. ♣

316 *Recycle Rex.*
GRADES: PS–2
DVD. Disney Educational, 2006, ISBN 978-1-59753-153-5, $49.95.
SUBJECTS: Recycling—Fiction

Dinosaurs, cartoons and singing = a fun and efficient way of delivering valuable lessons about recycling. In this ten-minute video by Disney Educational Products, Rex and his other dinosaur friends band together to save a local park from becoming a dump site. By learning to reuse and recycle, the group reduces the amount of waste their community produces. This short video uses humor and music to appeal to young children. ♲ ♣

NONFICTION

317 Barnham, Kay. *Recycle.*
GRADES: 1–3
SERIES: ENVIRONMENT ACTION! Crabtree Publishing, 2007, ISBN 978-0-7787-3659-2, 32p. $26.60.
SUBJECTS: Recycling

This book examines why it is important to recycle, how different materials are recycled, and how recycling can be done at home and at school. Like the other books in the Environment Action! series, this book features fast facts, easy-to-do tips, photographs, and vocabulary words. ♲ ☻

Barraclough, Sue.
SERIES: MAKING A DIFFERENCE. Sea-to-Sea

318 *Recycling Materials.*
GRADES: K–2
2008, ISBN 978-1-59771-108-1, 32p. $23.81.
SUBJECTS: Refuse and refuse disposal; Recycling

319 *Reducing Garbage.*
GRADES: K–2
2008, ISBN 978-1-59771-110-4, 32p. $23.81.
SUBJECTS: Refuse and refuse disposal; Waste minimization

320 *Respecting Our World.*
GRADES: K–2

2008, ISBN 978-1-59771-111-1, 32p. $23.81.
SUBJECTS: Environmental protection; Recycling

321 *Reusing Things.*
GRADES: K–2
2008, ISBN 978-1-59771-109-8, 32p. $23.81.
SUBJECTS: Environmental protection; Recycling

Photographs of smiling children doing their part to reduce, reuse, and recycle draw young readers into this helpful series. Each page gives fun and enticing ideas to help even the youngest environmentalist reduce the amount of waste produced in his or her home or community. The dynamic design, bright graphics, and easy-to-identify icons help readers navigate the pages and make this series an excellent choice for younger audiences. ♻ ☻

322 Bedford, Deborah Jackson. *Garbage Disposal.*
GRADES: 4–6
SERIES: ACTION FOR THE ENVIRONMENT. Smart Apple Media, 2006, ISBN 978-1-58340-595-6, 32p. $27.10.
SUBJECTS: Refuse and refuse disposal; Recycling

This book helps children understand that the things they throw away have to go somewhere. The short chapters explain that it is important to reduce waste by reusing and recycling as much as possible. The easy-to-understand text and "Action Stations" give young readers ideas to reduce the amount of garbage they produce. ♻ ☻

323 Borchers, Heidi. *Green Bling: Turning Bottles into Bangles.*
GRADES: 9–12
Leisure Arts, 2008, pap., ISBN 978-1-60140-635-4, 32p. $8.95.
SUBJECTS: Jewelry making; Recycling

A small book worth its weight in recycled gold. Definitely geared toward young adults, *Green Bling* will draw crafty readers in with the catchy title and keep them interested with the large photographs of the finished jewelry. The step-by-step instructions are detailed enough for crafting novices and include tips to help the reader construct cool and pretty "bling" from recycled material. ♻ 🎄

ACTIVITIES FOR OLDER ENVIRONMENTALISTS
✻ Hands-On Project ✻

Using recycled trash—including plastic bottles, toy parts, scrap paper, cardboard tubes, newspapers, cereal boxes, and magazines—allow students to create their own masterpieces. After reading one of the fiction titles listed in this book, encourage children to re-create a character or scene using your recycled trash. For older students, consider an altered clothing fashion show using recycled clothes, scissors, safety pins, fabric paint, and bleach. The following titles will help inspire you or your children:

Recycled Crafts Box (see entry 346)

Easy Earth-Friendly Crafts in 5 Steps (see entry 350)

AlternaCrafts: 20+ Hi-Style, Lo-Budget Projects to Make (see entry 361)

EcoArt! Earth-Friendly Art and Craft Experiences for 3- to 9-Year-Olds (see entry 370)

Everyday Art series by Gillian Chapman and Pam Robson (see entries 324–329)

Chapman, Gillian, and Pam Robson.
SERIES: EVERYDAY ART. PowerKids Press

324 *Making Art with Fabric.*
GRADES: 3–6
2008, ISBN 978-1-4042-3722-3, 32p. $25.25.
SUBJECTS: Handicrafts; Recycling

325 *Making Art with Packaging.*
GRADES: 3–6
2008, ISBN 978-1-4042-3724-7, 32p. $25.25.
SUBJECTS: Handicrafts; Recycling

326 *Making Art with Paper.*
GRADES: 3–6

2008, ISBN 978-1-4042-3725-4, 32p. $25.25.
SUBJECTS: Handicrafts; Paper; Recycling

327 *Making Art with Rocks and Shells.*
GRADES: 3–6
2008, ISBN 978-1-4042-3727-8, 32p. $25.25.
SUBJECTS: Recycling; Handicrafts

328 *Making Art with Sand and Earth.*
GRADES: 3–6
2008, ISBN 978-1-4042-3723-0, 32p. $25.25.
SUBJECTS: Recycling; Handicrafts

329 *Making Art with Wood.*
GRADES: 3–6
2008, ISBN 978-1-4042-3726-1, 32p. $25.25.
SUBJECTS: Recycling; Handicrafts

This inventive series is a treasure trove of ideas for crafts made from natural or recycled materials. Each book tackles a different medium, such as fabric, packaging, and wood. Some of the projects offer suggestions rather than instructions, leaving them open to the creativity of the readers. The results are unique and in most cases are quite beautiful—making them appealing to adults and younger readers alike. ♻ 🌳

Galko, Francine.
SERIES: EARTH FRIENDS. Heinemann

330 *Earth Friends at Home.*
GRADES: 1–3
2004, ISBN 978-1-4034-4895-8, 32p. $17.75.
SUBJECTS: Environmental protection; Energy conservation; Recycling

331 *Earth Friends at Play.*
GRADES: 1–3
2004, ISBN 978-1-4034-4896-5, 32p. $17.75.
SUBJECTS: Environmental protection; Recycling

332 *Earth Friends at School.*
GRADES: 1–3
2004, ISBN 978-1-4034-4897-2, 32p. $17.75.
SUBJECTS: Environmental protection; Recycling; Energy conservation

333 *Earth Friends at the Grocery Store.*
GRADES: 1–3
2004, ISBN 978-1-4034-4898-9, 32p. $17.75.
SUBJECTS: Environmental protection; Recycling

Children are invited to become "Earth friends" and to use natural resources more wisely in this series. Each book uses large photographs showing young children being environmentally responsible, combined with easy-to-understand graphics and text about the importance of recycling and conserving resources. Each book is packed with valuable information, a glossary, a bibliography, an index, and a hands-on activity. ♻ ☯ ♣

334 Ganeri, Anita. *Something Old, Something New: Recycling.*
GRADES: 3–5
SERIES: YOU CAN SAVE THE PLANET. Heinemann, 2005, ISBN 978-1-4034-6843-7, 32p. $19.75.
SUBJECTS: Recycling; Waste minimization

In an effort to truly involve the reader, this book provides case studies and "Taking Action" boxes that address why we need to reduce the amount of waste we produce. All books in the You Can Save the Planet series are excellent resources for young readers who want to understand the science behind environmental efforts such as recycling. ♻ ☯

335 Guillain, Charlotte. *Reusing and Recycling.*
GRADES: PS–2
SERIES: HELP THE ENVIRONMENT. Heinemann, 2008, ISBN 978-1-4329-0888-1, 24p. $20.71.
SUBJECTS: Recycling

Text that is easy to read and understand helps children identify with the need to reduce waste by reusing and recycling in this book in the Help the Environment series. Photographs show children taking steps to reuse and recycle materials. The simple picture glossary and index introduce young readers to research tools. ♻ ♣

336 Hall, Eleanor J. *Recycling.*
GRADES: 3–6
SERIES: OUR ENVIRONMENT. Kidhaven Press, 2004, ISBN 978-0-7377-1517-0, 48p. $26.20.

SUBJECTS: Recycling

The challenges and benefits of recycling—and what the future holds for re-cycling—are the focus of this book in the Our Environment series. The issues are examined using colorful diagrams, photographs, and well-placed defini-tions. Other helpful features include notes, a multimedia bibliography, a glossary, and indexes. 🌐

---

337 Hardy, Emma. *Green Crafts for Children: 35 Step-by-Step Projects Using Natural, Recycled, and Found Materials.*
GRADES: 3–6
Ryland Peters & Small, 2008, ISBN 978-1-906094-66-9, 128p. $19.95.
SUBJECTS: Handicrafts; Recycling

With chapters devoted to specific mediums such as salt dough, papier mache, paper recycling, and fabric, this sophisticated book is most likely intended for adults to use with children. However, the crafts are appropriate both for very young children (with assistance) and for older children and teens. Also, the clear steps with accompanying photographs will appeal to independent read-ers and teens, who will manage the text with ease. ♻ 🌳

Hewitt, Sally.
SERIES: GREEN TEAM. Crabtree Publishing

338 *Reduce and Reuse.*
GRADES: 2–5
2009, ISBN 978-0-7787-4095-7, 32p. $26.60.
SUBJECTS: Recycling; Waste minimization

339 *Waste and Recycling.*
GRADES: 2–5
2009, ISBN 978-0-7787-4098-8, 32p. $26.60.
SUBJECTS: Recycling; Refuse and refuse disposal

Part of the new Green Team series, these books emphasize the importance of reducing waste and reusing what we can. They also feature step-by-step instructions for environmental activities that young children can accomplish. Up-to-date statistics and scientific information are delivered in age-appro-priate language to ensure comprehension. ♻ 🌐

....

340 Inskipp, Carol. *Reducing and Recycling Waste.*
GRADES: 3–5
SERIES: IMPROVING OUR ENVIRONMENT. Gareth Stevens Publishing,
2005, ISBN 978-0-8368-4429-0, 32p. $19.50.
SUBJECTS: Refuse and refuse disposal; Recycling

This book in the Improving Our Environment series presents a clear look at
the current messy waste situation and how we got into it. Fact boxes and experiments provide statistical information and hands-on experiences to engage the reader. An evaluation of each of the different kinds of recyclable
materials is also an interesting feature. ♻ ◉

....

341 Knight, M. J. *Why Should I Recycle Garbage?*
GRADES: 2–4
SERIES: ONE SMALL STEP. Smart Apple Media, 2009, ISBN 978-1-
59920-267-9, 32p. $27.10.
SUBJECTS: Recycling

Readers will learn that even small actions can have big results in this entry
in the One Small Step series. Each two-page spread includes "I Can Make a
Difference" boxes with environmental tips and "One Small Fact" bubbles
about the importance of recycling. A glossary, a list of Web sites, and an
index are also included. ♻ ◉

....

342 Love, Ann, and Jane Drake. *Trash Action: A Fresh Look at Garbage.*
GRADES: 3–6
Ill. by Mark Thurman. Tundra Books, 2006, pap., ISBN 978-0-88776-
721-0, 76p. $14.95.
SUBJECTS: Refuse and refuse disposal; Recycling; Consumption

Readers who delve into this book's dense text will be rewarded with offbeat
information about how different cultures have dealt with the issue of trash.
The authors examine many different aspects of waste disposal, including recycling, consumerism, and pollution. The copious amount of text on each
page is enlivened with fun, inventive cartoons and pictures. An excellent
choice for serious environmentalists or those who are merely curious about
trash. ♻ ◉

ACTIVITIES FOR OLDER ENVIRONMENTALISTS
✳ Earth Friendly Crafts ✳

Additional Project: As a class, make recycled paper. A "recipe" for scratch-and-sniff recycled paper can be found in *Planet Earth: 25 Environmental Projects You Can Build Yourself* (see entry 270). Turn this project into a semi-annual one; encourage children to place their paper scraps—especially interestingly colored ones—in a box that will be used to make the recycled paper. Once the paper has been dried, use it to make nature journals.

SERIES: CARING FOR THE EARTH. Capstone Press

343 Mackenzie, Anne L. *Let's Recycle!*
GRADES: PS–2
2007, ISBN 978-0-7368-6323-0, 24p. $12.95.
SUBJECTS: Recycling; Refuse and refuse disposal

344 Nelson, Sara E. *Let's Reduce Garbage!*
GRADES: PS–2
2007, ISBN 978-0-7368-6324-7, 24p. $12.95.
SUBJECTS: Refuse and refuse disposal

345 Nelson, Sara E. *Let's Reuse!*
GRADES: PS–2
2007, ISBN 978-0-7368-6325-4, 24p. $12.95.
SUBJECTS: Conservation of natural resources; Refuse and refuse disposal

Large, bright photographs and basic text help introduce young children to the concepts of reducing, reusing, and recycling in these books in the Caring for the Earth series. Vocabulary terms, simple explanations, and useful, easy-to-do tips complement the text, as do photographs showing young children being environmentally responsible. A glossary, index, and small bibliography are also included, making these books excellent resources for the beginning reader and budding environmentalist. ♻ ◐

346 Martin, Laura C. *Recycled Crafts Box.*
GRADES: 2–4
Storey Publishing, 2003, ISBN 978-1-58017-523-4, 88p. $19.95.
SUBJECTS: Recycling; Handicrafts

The first chapter of this hands-on book discusses the negative impact that trash has on the Earth. Then the reader is in for a real treat: more than thirty inventive crafts made mostly from post-consumer recycled materials, such as a dancing tin-can man, rag coasters and bowls, and a "boot-iful" shoe garden. ♻ ☺ 🌳

347 Morgan, Sally. *Old Clothes.*
GRADES: 1–3
SERIES: DEALING WITH WASTE. Smart Apple Media, 2008, ISBN 978-1-59920-011-8, 30p. $27.10.
SUBJECTS: Handicrafts; Recycling

A look at various ways to dispose of old clothes—including reusing, recycling, donating to charity, and repurposing as new—this book also discusses footwear and eyewear. The importance of reducing waste and recycling everything possible is emphasized. Using colorful photographs and text boxes that draw attention to the waste in everyone's world, this book appeals to young readers. It includes a glossary, a bibliography, an index, and useful tips for reducing, reusing, and recycling. ♻ ☺

348 Morris, Neil. *Recycling.*
GRADES: K–3
SERIES: GREEN KIDS. QEB, 2008, ISBN 978-1-5956-6540-9, 24p. $24.25.
SUBJECTS: Recycling

Playful layouts and a generous amount of photographs add life to these books in the Green Kids series. Peppered throughout the text are relevant statistics about conservation that are easy for this age range to understand (for example, "5 energy-saving light bulbs use the same amount of electricity as 1 ordinary light bulb"). Quirky illustrations feature kid-friendly characters and arrows pointing out important information and there are "You Can Do It!" boxes. Includes an index. ♻ ☺ 🌳

349 Parks, Peggy J. *Garbage and Recycling.*
GRADES: 3–5
SERIES: RIPPED FROM THE HEADLINES: THE ENVIRONMENT. Erickson,
2008, ISBN 978-1-60217-023-0, 64p. $23.95.
SUBJECTS: Refuse and refuse disposal; Recycling

A balanced look at recycling's usefulness using charts, environmental vocabulary, photographs, and science concepts. Well-documented quotations
from a wide range of sources make this volume in the Ripped from the Headlines series unique. Includes a bibliography and an index. ⊙

350 Plomer, Anna Llimos. *Easy Earth-Friendly Crafts in 5 Steps.*
GRADES: 1–3
Enslow Publishers, 2008, ISBN 978-0-7660-3086-2, 32p. $22.60.
SUBJECTS: Handicrafts; Recycling

This creative book features fourteen originals crafts made from recycled materials that will provide children with hours of rainy-day fun. Each craft is
detailed on a two-page spread with color photographs demonstrating each
step. The directions are simple and easy to follow. Except for those requir-
ing scissors, these are crafts that even very young artists can master. ♻ ♟

Ridley, Sarah.
SERIES: HOW IT'S MADE. Gareth Stevens Publishing

351 *A Glass Jar.*
GRADES: 2–4
2007, ISBN 978-0-8368-6701-5, 32p. $24.00.
SUBJECTS: Glass manufacturing; Recycling

352 *A Metal Can.*
GRADES: 2–4
2007, ISBN 978-0-8368-6702-2, 32p. $24.00.
SUBJECTS: Metal manufacturing; Recycling

353 *A Paper Bag.*
GRADES: 2–4
2007, ISBN 978-0-8368-6703-9, 32p. $24.00.
SUBJECTS: Paper manufacturing; Recycling

354 *A Plastic Toy.*
GRADES: 2–4
2007, ISBN 978-0-8368-6704-6, 32p. $24.00.
SUBJECTS: Plastic manufacturing; Recycling

355 *A Rubber Tire.*
GRADES: 2–4
2007, ISBN 978-0-8368-6295-9, 32p. $24.00.
SUBJECTS: Rubber manufacturing; Recycling

The books in this series focus on the manufacturing of certain objects—specifically, how they are manufactured from recycled materials. The large text and photographs appeal to beginning readers and reluctant readers will delight in the machinery and technology. Vocabulary words appear in bold text and each book includes an index and a glossary. ●

356 Rodger, Ellen. *Recycling Waste.*
GRADES: 2–4
SERIES: SAVING OUR WORLD. Marshall Cavendish, 2008, ISBN 978-0-7614-3222-7, 32p. $28.50.
SUBJECTS: Refuse and refuse disposal; Recycling; Environmentalism

This book in the Saving Our World series uses vivid layouts, large photographs, and brief paragraphs to examine waste handling and the recycling process. The text explains the environmental and social impacts of recycling, with helpful waste-reducing tips and comprehension questions. ♺ ●

357 Ross, Kathy. *Earth-Friendly Crafts: Clever Ways to Reuse Everyday Items.*
GRADES: 2–4
Ill. by Celine Malepart. Millbrook Press, 2009, ISBN 978-0-8225-9099-6, 48p. $26.60.
SUBJECTS: Recycling; Handicrafts

Full of completely new crafts made from recycled objects, *Earth-Friendly Crafts* is perfect for art classes, libraries, and crafty kids. A combination of photographs and illustrations help to explain the steps involved in each project. Especially useful are the crafts that reuse otherwise nonrecyclable materials (such as toy cars and hair brushes). Some of the crafts are a bit far-fetched, but they certainly inspire creativity. ♺

358 Sivertsen, Linda, and Tosh Sivertsen. *Generation Green: The Ultimate Teen Guide to Living an Eco-Friendly Life.*

GRADES: 9–12

Simon Pulse, 2008, pap., ISBN 978-1-4169-6122-2, 272p. $10.99.

SUBJECTS: Environmental responsibility; Green movement; Sustainable living

An excellent guide for teenagers interested in leading more environmentally conscious lives. Quick paragraphs filled with practical tips focus on areas such as school, entertainment, and social activities. Written by a mother-and-son team, this book encourages teens to become involved in the environmental movement in any way they can. Also included are real-life "green teen" stories and an extensive multimedia bibliography that includes Web sites. ♺ ♁ ⚘

359 Spilsbury, Louise. *A Sustainable Future: Saving and Recycling Resources.*

GRADES: 3–6

SERIES: GEOGRAPHY FOCUS. Raintree Publishers, 2006, ISBN 978-1-4109-1117-9, 48p. $31.43.

SUBJECTS: Recycling; Conservation of natural resources

Why do we recycle? What does it mean to have a sustainable future? This book in the Geography Focus series will appeal to children's natural desire to help and may initiate further research on the subject. ♁

360 Turnbull, Stephanie. *Trash and Recycling.*

GRADES: PS–2

SERIES: USBORNE BEGINNERS: INFORMATION FOR YOUNG READERS: LEVEL 2. Ill. by Christyan Fox. Usborne Books, 2005, ISBN 978-0-7945-1073-2, 32p. $4.99.

SUBJECTS: Refuse and refuse disposal; Recycling

Though its cover is rather uninspiring, this book is a high-quality beginning reader with full-page color photographs, illustrations, and well-placed text. Helpful diagrams and numbered steps show the processes of composting and recycling. Also included are a glossary, an index, and Web sites. ♁

361 Vitkus, Jessica. *AlternaCrafts: 20+ Hi-Style, Lo-Budget Projects to Make.*
GRADES: 8–12
Stewart, Tabori, & Chang, 2005, ISBN 978-1-58479-456-1, 144p. $19.95.
SUBJECTS: Handicrafts; Recycling

Vitkus introduces her cool craft book by encouraging her readers to "recycle, recycle, recycle." Almost all of the clever crafts included in this book are made with recycled or recyclable material. Trendy and cute, the projects include crafts to wear, crafts for decorating, and crafts to give as gifts. The instructions are detailed and easy to follow, with varying levels of difficulty. This great addition to teen collections will appeal to both artists and environmentalists. ♺ 🌳

Walker, Kate.
SERIES: RECYCLE, REDUCE, REUSE, RETHINK. Smart Apple Media

362 *Aluminum.*
GRADES: 2–5
2004, ISBN 978-1-58340-559-8, 32p. $27.10.
SUBJECTS: Recycling; Aluminum

363 *Household Waste.*
GRADES: 2–5
2004, ISBN 978-1-58340-561-1, 32p. $27.10.
SUBJECTS: Recycling

364 *Paper.*
GRADES: 2–5
2004, ISBN 978-1-58340-558-1, 32p. $27.10.
SUBJECTS: Recycling; Paper

365 *Plastics.*
GRADES: 2–5
2004, ISBN 978-1-58340-556-7, 32p. $27.10.
SUBJECTS: Recycling; Plastics

366 *Steel.*
GRADES: 2–5
2004, ISBN 978-1-58340-560-4, 32p. $27.10.
SUBJECTS: Recycling; Steel

This series inspires action and investigation with its combination of hands-on tips and valuable environmental information. Photographs, charts, graphs, and fact boxes enliven the short chapters. As each title discusses how a material is recycled, there is also some examination of opposing viewpoints and community action. With an index and glossary in each book, this broad series of focused titles is a high-quality resource for any environmental collection. ♻ 🌐

---

367 Wilcox, Charlotte. *Earth-Friendly Waste Management.*
   GRADES: 3–5
   SERIES: SAVING OUR LIVING EARTH. Lerner Publishing, 2009, ISBN 978-0-8225-7560-3, 71p. $30.60.
   SUBJECTS: Refuse and refuse disposal; Recycling

A look at what people do with garbage, where garbage goes, and the recycling process. Real children and young adults working to improve the environment are featured. The detailed text, rich layouts, bold photographs, bibliography, index, and glossary are nice features that are included in all the books in the Saving Our Living Earth series. ♻ 🌐

---

368 Wilcox, Charlotte. *Recycling.*
   GRADES: 4–8
   SERIES: COOL SCIENCE. Lerner Publishing, 2008, ISBN 978-0-8225-6768-4, 48p. $26.60.
   SUBJECTS: Recycling

This book aims to make recycling hip—and succeeds! The chapter titles, including "Trashy Threads" and "What to Do with Doo-Doo" are both intriguing and relevant and are accentuated by neon-looking fonts and dynamic design. The tone of the chapter titles is continued throughout the book with subheadings such as "Zoo Poo" and "Pee Power." Do not let the wacky wording mislead you—the book is full of accurate and current information. 🌐 🏆

---

369 Young, Mitchell, ed. *Garbage and Recycling.*
   GRADES: 9–12
   SERIES: OPPOSING VIEWPOINTS. Greenhaven Press, 2007, ISBN 978-0-7377-3651-9, 256p. $37.40.

SUBJECTS: Refuse and refuse disposal; Recycling; Opposing viewpoints

Articles by authors of varied points of view address issues such as the benefits and drawbacks of recycling; landfills; e-waste; and the future of recycling. As in other Opposing Viewpoints books, *Garbage and Recycling* includes a bibliography and questions to prompt further discussion. 🌐

RECYCLED FAVORITES

370 Carlson, Laurie. *EcoArt! Earth-Friendly Art and Craft Experiences for 3- to 9-Year-Olds.*
GRADES: 3–6
Ill. by Loretta Trezzo Braren. Williamson Publishing, 1992, pap., ISBN 978-0-913589-68-7, 160p. $12.95.
SUBJECTS: Recycling; Handicrafts

There are no bells and whistles to this book filled with Earth-friendly crafts, but it's a tried-and-true environmental favorite. It features more than 100 crafts of different degrees of difficulty, ranging from homemade glue to egg-carton flowers. The black-and-white illustrations complement the easy-to-understand instructions. Although appropriate reading for grades 3 to 6, the crafts, as the subtitle indicates, are suitable for children as young as 3. There may be newer, flashier books, but this is one to keep on hand and use often. ♻ 🌳

371 Gibbons, Gail. *Recycle: A Handbook for Kids.*
GRADES: PS–2
Ill. by the author. Little, Brown, 1992, pap., ISBN 978-0-316-30943-1, 32p. $7.99.
SUBJECTS: Recycling

Gail Gibbons's cartoon illustrations complement her easy informational text to create a timeless book about recycling that appeals to younger readers. The recycling facts are still relevant and should remain so into the future. Gibbons's book should be valued for its simplicity and young-reader appeal. 🌐 🌳

372 Showers, Paul. *Where Does the Garbage Go?*
GRADES: 1–3
SERIES: LET'S-READ-AND-FIND-OUT SCIENCE. Ill. by Randy
Chewing. HarperCollins, 1994, ISBN 978-0-06-021054-0, 32p.
SUBJECTS: Refuse and refuse disposal; Recycling

This stage-two beginning reader looks at the past, present, and future of waste disposal. The easy-to-read text is accompanied by lively and colorful cartoons and explanatory graphics. Originally published in 1974 and reissued in 1994, this recycled favorite is still relevant (although it refers to recycling as "new") and a great recommendation for beginning independent readers or older readers with lower reading skills. The informative text also gives provides tips to reduce waste. ♻ ☻

GREEN PEOPLE

The following books include information on individuals who have had a direct impact on the history and future of the environmental movement.

SERIES: VOICES FOR GREEN CHOICES. Crabtree Publishing

373 Anderson, Dale. *Al Gore: A Wake-Up Call to Global Warming.*
GRADES: 3–6
2009, ISBN 978-0-7787-4666-9, 48p. $29.27.
SUBJECTS: Gore, Al; Environmentalists; Global warming

374 Callery, Sean. *Victor Wouk: Father of the Hybrid Car.*
GRADES: 3–6
2009, ISBN 978-0-7787-4664-5, 48p. $29.27.
SUBJECTS: Wouk, Victor; Environmentalists; Hybrid electric cars

375 Elliot, Henry. *John Muir: Protecting and Preserving the Environment.*
GRADES: 3–6
2009, ISBN 978-0-7787-4668-3, 48p. $29.27.
SUBJECTS: Muir, John; Environmentalists

376 Gazlay, Suzy. *David Suzuki: Doing Battle with Climate Change.*
GRADES: 3–6
2009, ISBN 978-0-7787-4665-2, 48p. $29.27.
SUBJECTS: Suzuki, David; Environmentalists; Climate change

377 Grayson, Robert. *Ed Begley, Jr.: Living Green.*
GRADES: 3–6
2009, ISBN 978-0-7787-4667-6, 48p. $29.27.
SUBJECTS: Begley, Ed, Jr.; Environmentalists

378 Lantier, Patricia. *Rachel Carson: Fighting Pesticides and Other Chemical Pollutants.*
GRADES: 3–6
2009, ISBN 978-0-7787-4663-8, 48p. $29.27.
SUBJECTS: Carson, Rachel; Environmentalists

The only current series devoted solely to environmental activists, Voices for Green Choices fills a gap in the resources for children on these heroes. Covering contemporary and well-known environmentalists such as David Suzuki, Al Gore, and Ed Begley, Jr., as well as historical environmentalists such as Rachel Carson and John Muir, this series also devotes a volume to Victor Wouk, the man called "Father of the Hybrid Car." Each book covers the subject's childhood, career, and importance to the environmental movement through photographs, anecdotes, and clearly written text. 🌍

379 Appelt, Kathi. *Miss Lady Bird's Wildflowers: How a First Lady Changed America.*
GRADES: 1–3
Ill. by Joy Fisher Hein. HarperCollins, 2005, ISBN 978-0-06-001107-9, 40p. $17.99.
SUBJECTS: Johnson, Lady Bird; Wildflowers; Environmental protection

This biography of Lady Bird Johnson tells the little-known tale of the former first lady's role in the foundation of the Wildflower Center in Austin, Texas. Young Lady Bird found comfort in the beautiful wildflowers found near her childhood home and this love continued throughout her life. She encouraged the passing of the Highway Beautification Act. This book is a delightfully told tale complemented with bright, lively, and descriptive illustrations. 🌍 🏆

380   Bang, Molly. *Nobody Particular: One Woman's Fight to Save the Bays.*

GRADES: 3–6

Ill. by the author. Henry Holt and Co., 2000, ISBN 978-0-8050-5396-8, 46p. $18.00.

SUBJECTS: Water pollution; Environmental protection; Chemical plants—Waste disposal

Bang tells the story of unlikely environmental activist Diane Wilson. Wilson, a Texas shrimper, fought with everything that she had to save her livelihood and her beloved bays from the chemical plants that were threatening them. The illustrations, newspaper clippings, and graphic novel format will appeal to younger and older readers alike. However, the dense text will be best appreciated by older readers. 🌍 🌳

381   Harmon, Daniel E. *Al Gore and Global Warming.*

GRADES: 7–10

SERIES: CELEBRITY ACTIVISTS. Rosen Publishing, 2008, ISBN 978-1-4042-1761-4, 112p. $33.25.

SUBJECTS: Gore, Al; Environmentalists; Global warming

Focusing on one of the most notable figures in today's environmental movement, this timely biography focuses on Gore's journey to prominence. By reading about his childhood and his life as a journalist and politician, readers will see what drove Gore to become a herald of the global warming crisis. 🌍

382   Jezer, Marty. *Rachel Carson: Biologist and Author.*

GRADES: 6–8

SERIES: AMERICAN WOMEN OF ACHIEVEMENT. Chelsea House, 1988, ISBN 978-1-55546-646-6, 112p.

SUBJECTS: Carson, Rachel; Biologists; Environmentalists

This 20-year-old but timeless biography takes a straightforward look at the life and legacy of Rachel Carson. The generous amount of factual information and black-and-white photographs make this a valuable resource for students. 🌍

383 Lasky, Kathryn. *John Muir: America's First Environmentalist.*
GRADES: 3–6
Ill. by Stan Fellows. Candlewick Press, 2006, ISBN 978-0-7636-1957-2, 41p. $16.99.
SUBJECTS: Muir, John; Naturalists; Conservationists

This book is the gently told life story of John Muir, founder of the Sierra Club and, as the title indicates, America's first environmentalist. Beginning with his childhood in Scotland and continuing into his years in America and Canada, excerpts from Muir's journals provide an account of his travels and appeal to a child's sense of wonder and adventure. The story is brought to life with Fellows's colorful and mild illustrations. The book includes enough factual information to make it a useful resource, but it is the gentle story line that will engage readers of all ages.
❂ ♈

384 Levine, Ellen. *Up Close: Rachel Carson.*
GRADES: 6–8
SERIES: UP CLOSE. Viking Children's, 2007, ISBN 978-0-670-06220-1, 224p. $15.99.
SUBJECTS: Carson, Rachel; Biologists; Environmentalists; Environmental Protection Agency

An intimate look at the legendary Rachel Carson. This detailed and anecdotal account tells Carson's story through quotations and relevant black-and-white photographs. Levine's gentle descriptions of Carson's struggle to overcome sex discrimination, political obstacles, family issues, and health problems bring to life the woman who is credited for the eventual formation of the Environmental Protection Agency. ❂

385 Malnor, Carol, and Bruce Malnor. *Earth Heroes: Champions of the Wilderness.*
GRADES: 8–12
Ill. by Anise C. Hovemann. Dawn Publications, 2009, pap., ISBN 978-1-58469-116-7, 144p. $11.95.
SUBJECTS: Thoreau, Henry David; Muir, John; Roosevelt, Theodore; Leopold, Aldo; St. Barbe Baker, Richard; Murie, Margaret; Suzuki, David; Maathai, Wangari

This is a compilation of biographies on environmental champions John Muir, Theodore Roosevelt, Henry David Thoreau, Aldo Leopold, Richard St. Barbe Baker, Margaret Murie, David Suzuki, and Wangari Maathai. These are in-depth profiles that address environmental impacts past and present. Each biography includes black-and-white photographs and pen-and-ink illustrations, and added to the end of each entry are timelines, fast facts, tips, and "ripples" about how that environmentalist's actions impacted others. This book is a one-of-a-kind resource that belongs in any middle/high school environmental collection. ♻ 🌐

386 Nivola, Claire. *Planting the Trees of Kenya: The Story of Wangari Maathai.*
GRADES: K–3
Ill. by the author. Farrar, Straus and Giroux, 2008, ISBN 978-0-374-39918-4, 32p. $16.95.
SUBJECTS: Maathai, Wangari; Green Belt Movement

Nobel Peace Prize winner Wangari Maathai was the founder of the Green Belt Movement. This picture book begins with Maathai as a young girl and emphasizes the importance of the adults in her life as driving forces behind her passion for conservation. The romantic prose and detailed watercolor illustrations follow Maathai as she inspires the Kenyan people to plant trees and restore the natural wonder of their land. This is an excellent read-aloud and includes more detailed biographical information following the story. 🌐 🌳

387 Winter, Jeanette. *Wangari's Trees of Peace: A True Story from Africa.*
GRADES: PS–2
Ill. by the author. Harcourt Children's Books, 2008, ISBN 978-0-15-206545-4, 32p. $17.00.
SUBJECTS: Maathai, Wangari; Green Belt Movement; Conservation of natural resources

When Wangari Maathai was a young child in Kenya, trees grew all around, but when she returned to her homeland as an adult, deforestation and development had made it unrecognizable. Simple, elegant, representational illustrations complement the uncomplicated text. This is a great book for read-alouds, storytimes, and beginning readers. ◐ ♟

GREEN THINGS

The following books are about the environmental movement and the policies and the organizations that affect the environment.

388 Adair, Rick, ed. *Critical Perspectives on Politics and the Environment.*
GRADES: 9–12
SERIES: SCIENTIFIC AMERICAN CRITICAL ANTHOLOGIES ON ENVIRONMENT AND CLIMATE. Rosen Publishing, 2006, ISBN 978-1-4042-0823-0, 224p. $31.95.
SUBJECTS: Environmentalism; Environmental policy

The books in this series consist of collections of *Scientific American* articles originally published between 1995 and 2005 that relate to the environmental movement. Most of the articles include black-and-white graphics such as diagrams, charts, and illustrations to complement the text. High school students will find these useful for reports about the environmental movement and politics. ◐

389 Calhoun, Yael. *Environmental Policy.*
GRADES: 9–12
SERIES: ENVIRONMENTAL ISSUES. Chelsea House, 2005, ISBN 978-0-7910-8205-8, 164p. $31.95.
SUBJECTS: Environmental policy

Each book in this series takes an in-depth look at an environmental issue and how it is related to other environmental concerns. These books use academic language and do not include charts, graphics, or photographs. Each chapter includes articles written by different authors to provide varied perspectives. Bibliographies and extensive indexes add to this series' value as a research resource for high school collections. ♺ ◐

390 Greenland, Paul R., and AnnaMarie L. Sheldon. *Career Opportunities in Conservation and the Environment.*
GRADES: 9–12
SERIES: CAREER OPPORTUNITIES IN. Checkmark Books, 2008, pap., ISBN 978-0-8160-6742-8, 320p. $18.95.
SUBJECTS: Conservation of natural resources—Vocational guidance; Ecology—Vocational guidance

Perfect for career centers, high schools, and libraries, this is an excellent resource for budding environmentalists. More than sixty-five career profiles are included, with information about the skills and education required for each job. Each career description is extremely detailed and includes salary information and employment prospects. The appendices round off this book with information on educational institutions and professional and governmental agencies associated with environmental efforts. ⊕

391 Harmon, Daniel E. *The Environmental Protection Agency.*
GRADES: 6–9
SERIES: YOUR GOVERNMENT: HOW IT WORKS. Chelsea House, 2002, ISBN 978-0-7910-6792-5, 64p. $25.00.
SUBJECTS: Environmental Protection Agency; Environmental policy

One of the few books for teens dedicated solely to this organization, this volume addresses the history, scope, and necessity of the Environmental Protection Agency. Though it could use updating, this entry in the Your Government series is a valuable resource for research on environmental policy, and it includes helpful illustrations and photographs. ⊕

392 Parry, Ann. *Greenpeace.*
GRADES: 5–8
Chelsea House, 2005, ISBN 978-0-7910-8815-9, 32p. $22.95.
SUBJECTS: Greenpeace; Environmentalism

Readers learn about the history and values of Greenpeace before delving into the organization's achievements and people. Each Greenpeace concern is allotted a full page that discusses related campaigns. The book is also full of colorful photographs, "Did You Know?" features, and defined terms. 🌏

---

393 Sonneborn, Liz. *The Environmental Movement: Protecting Our Natural Resources.*
GRADES: 5–7
SERIES: REFORM MOVEMENTS IN AMERICAN HISTORY. Chelsea House, 2008, ISBN 978-0-7910-9537-9, 128p. $32.50.
SUBJECTS: Environmentalism

Follow the path of the environmental movement from the days of Rachel Carson and John Muir to today's environmental activism. The chronological chapters focus on the people, events, and legislation that have affected the environmental movement. Text boxes provide more in-depth information on landmark cases and people and the timeline, index, and bibliography help students with their research. A very useful resource to complete your environmental collection. 🌏

EARTH DAY

The following books are about Earth Day, its history, why it's important, and how it is celebrated.

Fiction

394 Mayer, Mercer. *It's Earth Day.*
GRADES: PS–2
SERIES: THE NEW ADVENTURES OF LITTLE CRITTER. Ill. by the author. HarperFestival, 2008, pap., ISBN 978-0-06-053959-7, 24p. $3.99.
SUBJECTS: Earth Day—Fiction

On Earth Day, Little Critter's teacher shows the class a film that opens Little Critter's eyes to environmental concerns. With his characteristic enthusiasm and goofiness, Little Critter sets out to change his habits and those of his family and friends. Full of great environmental tips, this is a fun picture book that is sure to please both those who are familiar with Little Critter and those who are not. ♻ 🌳

395 Murphy, Stuart. *Earth Day—Hooray!*
GRADES: PS–2
SERIES: MATHSTART 3. Ill. by Renee Andriani. HarperCollins, 2004, ISBN 978-0-06-000127-8, 40p. $16.99.
SUBJECTS: Recycling—Fiction; Earth Day—Fiction; Mathematics—Fiction

This clever little picture book not only contains a lively story and illustrations, but is also full of environmental tips and math practice. It features a group of children who work together to collect 5,000 aluminum cans. The colorful cartoon illustrations move the story along and the book ends with math and comprehension questions. 🌍 🌳

396 Schnetzler, Pattie. *Earth Day Birthday.*
GRADES: PS–2
Ill. by Chad Wallace. Dawn Publications, 2004, pap., ISBN 978-1-58469-054-2, 32p. $8.95.
SUBJECTS: Earth Day—Fiction; Songs and music

Based on "The Twelve Days of Christmas," this picture book is entertaining and energetic. The full-page illustrations feature animals mentioned in the text. Catchy and clever, with definite storytime possibilities, this book also offers information about Earth Day, environmental tips, and a score set to the tune. ♻ 🌳

Nonfiction

397 Aloian, Molly. *Earth Day.*
GRADES: PS–2
SERIES: CELEBRATIONS IN MY WORLD. Crabtree Publishing, 2009, ISBN 978-0-7787-4288-3, 32p. $26.60.
SUBJECTS: Earth Day

The most current and comprehensive resource for this age group, this book has wide appeal. Young readers will appreciate the large format, text, and photographs, and educators will appreciate that the book covers the history of Earth Day, how to get involved, and legislation that has affected the environment. Boldface vocabulary words, a glossary, and an index are included. ♻ 🌍

398 Lowery, Linda. *Earth Day.*
GRADES: 2–4
SERIES: ON MY OWN HOLIDAYS. Ill. by Mary Bergherr. Lerner
Publishing, 2004, ISBN 978-1-57505-700-2, 48p. $25.26.
SUBJECTS: Earth Day; Environmental protection; Nelson, Gaylord

An easy reader about the history of Earth Day—from its beginnings
through today. Also covered is the role that Senator Gaylord Nelson
played in the creation of the holiday and his fight to raise awareness of
environmental issues. The clear, simple text is accompanied by color illustrations. This book is a nice introduction to environmentalism with
many helpful tips for budding environmentalists. ✿ ●

399 Nelson, Robin. *Earth Day.*
GRADES: PS–2
SERIES: FIRST STEP NONFICTION. Lerner Publishing, 2003, ISBN
978-0-8225-1283-7, 23p. $18.60.
SUBJECTS: Earth Day; Environmentalism; Environmental
protection

The First Step Nonfiction series eases beginning readers into nonfiction
subject matter. Each page in this book about Earth Day features one
short sentence in large text, vocabulary words in bold text, and a large
color photograph relating to Earth Day activities. ●

400 Trueit, Trudi Strain. *Earth Day.*
GRADES: PS–2
SERIES: ROOKIE READ-ABOUT HOLIDAYS. Children's Press, 2007,
ISBN 978-0-531-12455-0, 32p. $20.50.
SUBJECTS: Earth Day; Environmentalism

This Rookie Reader packs in more information than other books for this
reading level. With evocative phrases ("imagine a city where the air is
so dirty it is hard to breathe") and powerful pictures, this book engages
the reader's imagination. Beginning reader features include large text,
pronunciation hints, large photographs, and a helpful "Words You
Know" section. ●

RECYCLING STORYTIME

Begin with "Good Morning, Dear Earth."

Good morning, dear Earth
Good morning, dear Sun (hold your hands above your head)
Good morning, dear stones (put a "stone" in your hand)
And the flowers, every one. (make your hand into a flower)

Good morning, dear bees (fly a "bee" around between your fingers)
And the birds in the trees (make your arms into wings and flap them)
Good morning to you (point to the children)
And good morning to me. (point to yourself)

"Good morning, children. Today we are going to talk and read books about recycling, reducing, and reusing. Does anyone know what it means to recycle? Let's read a book to find out more about it!"

Read *Michael Recycle* by Ellie Bethel (see entry 305).

"That had a lot of helpful information about recycling. There are so many things that we can recycle!"

Bring out a bag of items that children will recognize such as water bottles, juice boxes, glass jars, and paper and plastic bags.

"Let's look for the 'recycle' symbol on these items to see if they can be recycled. I can't find a recycle symbol on the plastic bag. We should take reusable cloth bags to the store instead of using these plastic ones that can't be recycled. Let's sing a song to help us remember."

Sing "Five Plastic Bags" (to the tune of "Five Little Ducks Went Out to Play").

Five plastic bags blowing in the breeze
On the ground and in the trees
If we use a cloth bag instead of these
There will be four plastic bags blowing in the breeze.

(Continue to count down until you reach "NO plastic bags blowing in the breeze")

"When we recycle, we turn one thing into something else. There are lots of different ways to do that. This next book tells the story of some creative children who recycle in a very imaginative way."

Read *The Dumpster Diver* by Janet S. Wong (see entry 313).

"Reduce, reuse, and recycle: These words all start with the letter R."

Play "3 R's" by Jack Johnson (see entry 315).

"We have one more book that is about reusing."

Read *Joseph Had a Little Overcoat* by Simms Taback (see entry 310).

"Another way you can reuse your clothing is to give it to Goodwill or the Salvation Army so other people can use it. So, before you buy something, see if you will be able to recycle it or reuse it when you are finished with it. Thank you for coming to storytime today, I hope you remember to love our Earth by reducing waste, reusing, and recycling."

Sing "If You Love Earth and You Know It" (to the tune of "If You're Happy and You Know It").

If you love Earth and you know it, clap your hands!
If you love Earth and you know it, clap your hands!
If you love Earth and you know it, then let your actions show it!
If you love Earth and you know it, clap your hands!

Second verse: If you love Earth and you know it, stomp your feet!

Third verse: If you love Earth and you know it, shout "Reduce!"
If you love Earth and you know it, shout "Reuse!"
If you love Earth and you know it, then let your actions show it!
If you love Earth and you know it, shout "Recycle!"

CONSERVATION

CONSERVATION IS ESSENTIAL. OUR RESOURCES ARE limited and it is important to protect those that remain for future generations. Children and teens *are* those future generations, so it is only appropriate that we give them the tools to start protecting the environment that they will inherit.

The titles in the previous chapters help children understand the different components of our fragile Earth and what happens when we mistreat it. The 3 Rs are a good foundation for environmental action, but conservation is about more than reducing, reusing, and recycling, and therefore many of the books included in this chapter contain broader information about the environment. *Conservation* can seem an abstract concept to a young child so books for young children about conservation ask children to do what comes naturally: To look at the world in wonder. These books allow children to identify with things in nature that make them happy, and help readers understand that they have a responsibility to look after these things. Often these books use photographs or illustrations of young children participating in environmentally friendly behavior in order for the child to relate with the behavior. Picture books may use personification to make animals, plants, and even the Earth more familiar to children.

Older children and teens readily understand concepts and realize that conservation is not only an action but also a way of life. Books for these audiences touch on all the issues that affect the Earth—pollution, deforestation, overpopulation, biodiversity, and so forth. These books also provide environmental tips and contacts for associations and organizations that help children and teens get involved. Since conservation is needed around the world, many of the titles in this chapter address global concerns as well.

Titles included in this chapter often contain a little bit of everything. Sometimes they don't fit into any of the previous chapters—they fit into *all* of them. Conservation is not just about recycling; it is about every choice that we make that is a conscious effort to help our environment. We hope these efforts will become as ingrained as breathing.

FICTION

401 Cherry, Lynne. *The Sea, the Storm, and the Mangrove Tangle.*
GRADES: 1–3
Ill. by the author. Farrar, Straus and Giroux, 2004, ISBN 978-0-374-36482-3, 40p. $16.00.
SUBJECTS: Ecology—Fiction; Mangrove swamps—Fiction; Marine animals—Fiction

Lynne Cherry fictionalizes the mangrove tangle and the animals that depend on it for their survival. By personifying the animals, Cherry helps the readers understand that the mangrove tree serves many purposes and that its survival is necessary to conserve the natural environment of many, many animals. The illustrations are colorful, detailed, and bring a lively movement to the story. Though the personification is fiction, the detailed illustrations and the message are accurate and a great way to introduce the importance of ecosystem conservation. 🌳

402 Child, Lauren. *What Planet Are You From, Clarice Bean?*
GRADES: 1–3
Candlewick Press, 2002, ISBN 978-0-7636-1696-0, 32p. $16.99.
SUBJECTS: Environmental protection—Fiction; School—Fiction

Misunderstood Clarice Bean becomes an eco-warrior in this entertaining picture book. Child's familiar non-linear text, illustrations, and collage layouts depict a Clarice burdened by a school project on the environment. The project is rescued by her brother's determination to save a neighborhood tree. A funny picture book perfect for young independent readers. 🌳

403 Cole, Henry. *On Meadowview Street.*
GRADES: PS–2
Ill. by the author. Greenwillow Books, 2007, ISBN 978-0-06-056482-7, 30p. $17.99.
SUBJECTS: Nature—Fiction; Gardeners and gardening—Fiction

When Caroline moves onto Meadowview Street there is no meadow to view, so she decides to change this. She begins by saving a wildflower in her yard and soon her entire yard becomes a wildflower preserve complete with trees, birdhouses, and even a pond. The neighbors take a cue from her and the street finally comes to resemble its namesake. Henry Cole's fun story and cute, colorful illustrations are sure to inspire gardeners young and old. 🌳

---

404 Cole, Sheila. *The Canyon.*
GRADES: 4–6
HarperCollins, 2002, ISBN 978-0-06-029496-0, 160p. $15.95.
SUBJECTS: Conservation of natural resources—Fiction; Environmental protection—Fiction; Real estate development—Fiction

Zach enjoys hiking and taking photographs of the canyon near his family's home. When he discovers that a company plans to turn the canyon into a luxury housing development, he decides to fight the corporation in any way he can. This well-written, gripping story will appeal to nature enthusiasts and budding activists, as well as all fiction readers. 🌳

---

405 Collard, Sneed B., III. *Flash Point.*
GRADES: 7–10
Peachtree Publishers, 2006, ISBN 978-1-56145-385-6, 214p. $15.95.
SUBJECTS: Ecology—Fiction; Deforestation—Fiction; Nature—Effect of human beings on—Fiction

High school sophomore Luther's life is already in flux since quitting the football team when he begins to hang out with another social outsider, Alex. As Alex and he team up and create the Student Forest Society, Luther's other relationships become more and more strained, to the point of violence. While Luther feels he is doing the right thing, he must decide if it is worth alienating his friends and family. Environmentalism partners with a coming-of-age story to make this novel intriguing and realistic. 🌳

---

406 Colman, Michelle Sinclair. *Eco Babies Wear Green.*
GRADES: BABIES–PS
Ill. by Nathalie Dion. Tricycle Press, 2008, ISBN 978-1-58246-253-0, $6.95.
SUBJECTS: Infants—Fiction; Environmental responsibility—Fiction

This board book is perfect for babies who are the green apples of their parents' eyes. Cute and colorful illustrations show trendy little babies being environmentally friendly without even trying. The simple sentences each begin with "Eco babies . . . " and end with all the ways that people can help to save the environment. Though parents may delight in it more than the intended audience, this is a fun book nonetheless. 🌳

407 Delaney, Mark. *The Kingfisher's Tale.*
GRADES: 4–6
SERIES: MISFITS, INC. Topeka Bindery, 2000, ISBN 978-0-613-85287-6, 217p. $14.40.
SUBJECTS: Environmental protection—Fiction; Mystery stories—Fiction

On a trip to a national forest, the Misfits—four high school teens—find themselves in the middle of an ecological mystery. Threatened Kingfisher birds are dying in the forest, and the Misfits realize this is a scandal involving people with political influence. This is a great recommendation for anyone, even those unfamiliar with the Misfits series, and especially reluctant readers. 🌳

408 Gliori, Debi. *The Trouble with Dragons.*
GRADES: PS–2
Ill. by the author. Bloomsbury, 2008, ISBN 978-0-7475-9540-3, 32p. $15.95.
SUBJECTS: Conservation of natural resources—Fiction; Environmental protection—Fiction

In this cautionary fairy tale told in rhyming text, dragons create an uninhabitable Earth by polluting, chopping down trees, and contributing to global warming with their fire breath. The damage they cause is reminiscent of humans' impact on the Earth. The story is quick, lively, and not too scary, with illustrations that really bring it to life. Gliori's playful dragons live in a colorful world until their woeful ignorance zaps the color and wildlife from nature. A must-have for environmental preschool storytimes or reading circles, this picture book has child and adult appeal. 🌳

409 Gould, Peter. *Write Naked.*
GRADES: 9–12

Farrar, Straus and Giroux, 2008, ISBN 978-0-374-38483-8, 256p. $16.95.

SUBJECTS: Writing—Fiction; Global warming—Fiction

Victor is a 16-year-old budding writer whose adage is "you have to be naked to write." An interesting relationship develops when a teenage girl who lives near Victor's uncle's cabin discovers his experiment. Rose Anna is a free-spirited nature lover, who also happens to be quite attractive to Victor. Told in stream-of-consciousness short chapters and through the environmental fantasy that the teenagers create, this is a funny and honest coming-of-age story that should appeal to both boys and girls. 🌳

---

410 Green, Jen. *Why Should I Protect Nature?*

GRADES: PS–2

SERIES: WHY SHOULD I? Ill. by Mike Gordon. Barron's Educational, 2005, pap., ISBN 978-0-7641-3154-7, 32p. $6.99.

SUBJECTS: Conservation of natural resources—Fiction

Perfect for young readers, this book delivers information in a story that kids can easily identify with, illustrated with multicultural cartoon characters. The text is large and describes the environmental actions—of which there are many—that appear throughout the book. A great choice for independent readers, this book is also helpful for parents and teachers, with tips for reading this book with children and follow-up activities. This series is highly recommended and should remain a timely resource for initiating conversations with children about environmental issues. ♻ 🌍 🌳

---

411 Harper, Charise Mericle. *Just Grace Goes Green.*

GRADES: 3–6

SERIES: JUST GRACE. Houghton Mifflin, 2009, ISBN 978-0-618-95957-0, 192p. $16.00.

SUBJECTS: Friendship—Fiction; Recycling—Fiction; Sustainable living—Fiction

Grace directs her empathy toward the environment in this fourth installment in the Just Grace series. When Miss Lois's class goes green, Grace and her friend Mimi jump into the project full force. Readers will enjoy the humor and the amusing black-and-white cartoons. Conservation tips and terms are integrated so smoothly throughout that children won't even realize how much information is packed into this delightful book. ♻ 🌍 🌳

412 Herzog, Brad. *S Is for Save the Planet: A How-to-Be-Green Alphabet.*
GRADES: PS–4
Ill. by Linda Ayriss. Sleeping Bear Press, 2009, ISBN 978-1-58536-428-2, 40p. $17.95.
SUBJECTS: Environmental protection—Fiction

This beautiful picture book is an excellent read-aloud as well as an informative resource. Each colorful page boasts realistic illustrations overlaid by rhyming text perfect for young, independent readers or for reading aloud. Tons of conservation ideas and scientific information aid activists and researchers. The back of the book has a list of relevant Web resources aimed at children. ♺ ❸ ❦

413 Hiaasen, Carl. *Hoot.*
GRADES: 4–6
Knopf, 2002, ISBN 978-0-375-82181-3, 304p. $16.95.
SUBJECTS: Environmental protection—Fiction; Burrowing owls—Fiction

An identifiable protagonist and cast of oddball characters make Hiaasen's first novel for younger readers a hit for all ages. Roy is used to moving, but his new home in Coconut Grove, Florida, presents new challenges—including the small owls whose home is threatened by development. Roy and his friends work, with many humorous complications, to save the owls and fight the adults who just don't seem to understand. Children will identify with Roy's plight and appreciate the mystery and humor characteristic of Hiaasen's work. ❦

414 Hiaasen, Carl. *Scat.*
GRADES: 4–6
Knopf, 2009, ISBN 978-0-375-83486-8, 384p. $16.99.
SUBJECTS: Wildlife conservation—Fiction

The latest eco-tale from Hiaasen features the usual trappings. When a biology teacher disappears, Nick and Marta investigate the mystery. Full of crazy characters, a slimy oilman, and a family of endangered panthers, Hiaasen's book contains eco- and social consciousness and will appeal to humor and mystery fans alike. ❦

415 Koss, Amy Goldman. *Kailey.*
GRADES: 2–4
SERIES: AMERICAN GIRL TODAY. American Girl, 2003, pap., ISBN 978-1-58485-591-0, 160p. $6.95.
SUBJECTS: Tide pools—Fiction; Environmental protection—Fiction; Real estate development—Fiction

The American Girl Today series transports the popular books and dolls into the present. Kailey is a boogie-boarding, beach-loving girl who leads a fairly carefree life. She's excited about the new mega-movie theater that is planned for the beach until she realizes her beloved tide pools are going to be destroyed in the process. This motivates her into action, and the readers go along for the ride. This book is sure to be a hit with American Girl fans, but is solid enough to recommend on its own merits. Like most American Girl books, it provides some informational material in the backmatter, including a story of a real-life girl very similar to Kailey who was motivated to make a difference in her community. 🌳

416 Lorbiecki, Marybeth. *Paul Bunyan's Sweetheart.*
GRADES: PS–2
Ill. by Renee Graef. Sleeping Bear Press, 2007, ISBN 978-1-58536-289-9, 29p. $16.95.
SUBJECTS: Bunyan, Paul; Nature—Effect of human beings on—Fiction; Environmental degradation—Fiction; Deforestation—Fiction

Everyone knows the story of giant Paul Bunyan of lumberjack fame, but his tale probably does not sit well with the environmentally conscious. This lovely picture book solves that moral dilemma with the tale of Paul Bunyan's sweetheart who showed him the error of his ways. Giantess Lucette's love of the land inspires Bunyan to become a forester, planting trees for all the trees he chopped down. The illustrations are big, bold, and full of expression and complement the story nicely. 🌳

417 Pfitsch, Patricia Curtis. *Riding the Flume.*
GRADES: 5–8
Simon & Schuster, 2002, ISBN 978-0-689-83823-1, 240p. $16.95.
SUBJECTS: Conservation of natural resources—Fiction; Giant Sequoia—Fiction; Logging—Fiction

This book takes place in 1894, when the giant trees of what is now Sequoia National Park were being cut down for lumber. Fifteen-year-old Francie discovers a mysterious note left by her dead sister Carrie in a hole in one of the ancient sequoias. The note leads her on an adventure to save the oldest of the trees before it is too late. Pfitsch delivers a nice environmental mystery with a dash of adventure. 🌳

---

418   Ray, Jane. *The Apple-Pip Princess.*
GRADES: PS–2
Ill. by the author. Candlewick Press, 2008, ISBN 978-0-7636-3747-7, 32p. $16.99.
SUBJECTS: Conservation of natural resources—Fiction; Princesses—Fiction

This sweet fairy tale tells the story of a hard kingdom that loses its beauty along with its natural resources. It takes the work of an overlooked princess to bring back its beauty by planting all kinds of fruit and vegetables and restoring the kingdom's natural resources. Perfect for storytime, the book's illustrations are lively, delicate, and detailed, integrating collage and watercolor. A great choice, especially for princess fans, but even non-princess types will enjoy this fairy tale. 🌳

---

419   Schaefer, Carole Lexa. *Cool Time Song.*
GRADES: PS–2
Ill. by Pierr Morgan. Viking, 2005, ISBN 978-0-670-05928-7, 32p. $15.99.
SUBJECTS: Nature conservation—Fiction; Savannah animals—Fiction

An excellent read-aloud, this picture book is a whimsical ode to African animals and their environments. Schaefer's onomatopoetic words dance and sing across the page and invite little voices to participate in the experience of the book and in the care of the earth. The illustrations pop from the page and move right along with the words in an explosion of color. The message is subtle and clear, and is strengthened by the book's energy. 🌳

---

420   Tate, Nikki. *Trouble on Tarragon Island.*
GRADES: 4–7
SERIES: TARRAGON ISLAND. Topeka Bindery, 2006, ISBN 978-1-4177-4796-2, 216p. $18.70.

SUBJECTS: Environmental protection—Fiction

This third installment in the series moves fast, and each chapter opens with a relevant quotation from a notable person in history. If children can can move past the pretty horrible cover art (and let's face it, middle schoolers aren't too forgiving when it comes to the cover of a book), the story is intriguing and funny at times. Heather Blake's grandmother is one of a group of women so dedicated to saving a local habitat from destruction that they produce a semi-nude calendar to raise awareness. Heather must get past her humiliation to examine her grandmother's motivation and determine that she wants to carry on in her granny's footsteps. 🌳

421 Walsh, Melanie. *10 Things I Can Do to Help My World: Fun and Easy Eco-Tips.*
GRADES: PS–1
Ill. by the author. Candlewick Press, 2008, ISBN 978-0-7636-4144-3, 40p. $17.50.
SUBJECTS: Waste minimization—Fiction; Energy conservation—Fiction

This helpful picture book is made from 100 percent recycled material and that is just the beginning of this unique book's efficiency. Told from the point of view of a child, the large text describes ten easy-to-do environmental steps that even the youngest reader can take. Smaller text explains why these tasks are helpful. The layout invites readers to turn the shaped pages by offering suspended sentences that are answered on the following page. This is a delightful read-aloud and a good choice for newly independent readers.

WATCHING AND LISTENING GREEN

422 Cardon, Sam, and Jerry Williams. *We Can Save Our Planet.*
GRADES: PS–6
CD. Classroom Classics, $15.00.
SUBJECTS: Environmental protection—Songs and music; Songs and music

Classroom Classics produces high-quality CDs that can be used in classroom teaching or to present musical programs. The simple, clear, and meaningful lyrics are accompanied by a powerful, moving score and full orchestra. *We Can Save Our Planet* includes eleven songs (including a rap!) that both teach and motivate children about environmental subjects. Included are upbeat and lively songs such as "Goin' Green," "A Bad Situation," and "Bring It Back, Jack." Slower songs including "We Can Save Our Planet" and "If We Hold on Together" add diversity to the song list. Instrumental versions of each song can be used in music classes or performances. Includes booklet with lyrics. 🌳

423   Kallis, Coco. *Environmental Songs for Kids.*
GRADES: PS–2
CD. Smithsonian Folkways Recordings, 1999.
SUBJECTS: Songs and music; Ecology

Each song on this CD is dedicated to informing children about environmental issues and encouraging them to participate in conserving our natural resources. Coco Kallis's lead vocals are easy to understand and entice children to sing along. Mostly folksy, the CD also features songs with bluegrass, calypso, and blues styling, and ranging from the upbeat and lively to gentle and contemplative. Also included is a booklet with lyrics, song information, conservation tips, and environmental discussion questions. 🌳

Lewis, Christopher, and Linda Lewis.
SERIES: ECO-KIDS ELEMENTARY. Landmark Media

424   *The Earth Needs Your Help.*
GRADES: 2–5
DVD. 2008, $195.
SUBJECTS: Environmental responsibility

425   *How "Eco" Are You?*
GRADES: 2–5
DVD. 2008, $195.
SUBJECTS: Environmental responsibility

426   *The Things You Can Do.*
GRADES: 2–5
DVD. 2008, $195.00.
SUBJECTS: Environmental responsibility

A three-part series geared toward elementary students and narrated by young teenagers. In the first program, "The Earth Needs Your Help," clips and animated diagrams explain the challenges facing the environment. This sets up "How "Eco" Are You?" which asks viewers to examine their homes, schools, communities, and lifestyles to determine how environmentally friendly they are. The final part, "The Things You Can Do," provides many useful tips. Each program is approximately 15 minutes long and will motivate viewers while it reinforces scientific and environmental information. ♺ ☯

Lewis, Christopher, and Linda Lewis.
SERIES: ECO-KIDS MIDDLE SCHOOL. Landmark Media

427 *The Earth Needs Your Help.*
GRADES: 6–9
DVD. 2008, $195.
SUBJECTS: Environmental responsibility

428 *How "Eco" Are You?*
GRADES: 6–9
DVD. 2008, $195.
SUBJECTS: Environmental responsibility

429 *The Things You Can Do.*
GRADES: 6–9
DVD. 2008, $195.
SUBJECTS: Environmental responsibility

Like the Eco-Kids Elementary series (see entries 424–426), this three-part series for middle school students looks at the challenges facing the environment; urges viewers to explore their homes, schools, communities, and lifestyles to determine how environmentally friendly they are; and discusses measures young people can take to improve the world around them. Each program is approximately fifteen minutes long and will motivate viewers while it reinforces scientific and environmental information. ♺ ☯

430 McKhool, Chris. *Earth, Seas, and Air.*
GRADES: PS–6

CD. McKhool (SOCAN), 1996, $15.00.
SUBJECTS: Environmental protection—Songs and music; Songs and music

Chris McKhool's enthusiasm for both music and the environment is evident in his work. *Earth, Seas, and Air* is a musical adventure packed with fourteen phenomenal songs that both children and adults will love. Using a combination of spoken words and clear vocals, the concepts and stories featured are understandable for younger audiences but will be appreciated by all ages. The catchy tunes include the catchy "B Is for Bicycle" and "No More Trash," mellow tunes "Mother Earth" and "Sing for the Forests," and environmental music masterpieces "Rivers, Lakes, and Seas" and "Web of Life." No environmental collection is complete without this CD. Includes booklet with lyrics. ♻ ◐ ♣

431 Raffi. *Evergreen Everblue.*
GRADES: PS–2
CD. Shoreline/MCA/Troubador, 1996, $14.98.
SUBJECTS: Environmental protection; Songs and music

This CD features mostly original songs with some "recycled favorites" such as "One Light, One Sun." All of them offer messages of ecology and sustainability. With Raffi's characteristic beats and clear lyrics, children and adults alike can sing along to these environmental tunes. Raffi's songs manage to be both gentle and upbeat and are time-honored favorites. Also available on www.raffinews.com is a free download of "Cool It," a song about global warming. ♣

Rouse, Joyce Johnson (Earth Mama).
Rouse House Music

432 *Around the World.*
GRADES: PS–6
CD. 1997, $15.00.
SUBJECTS: Environmental protection—Songs and music; Songs and music

433 *Christmas Heart.*
GRADES: PS–6
CD. $15.00.

SUBJECTS: Environmental protection—Songs and music; Songs and music

434 *Grass Roots.*
GRADES: PS–6
CD. $15.00.
SUBJECTS: Environmental protection—Songs and music; Songs and music

Crisp, sweet, yet soulful vocals are the highlight of Earth Mama's fun CDs, and these vocals are accompanied by diverse and interesting beats and poignant environmental lyrics. The *Around the World* CD has global spice, and each environmentally centered song—such as "Energy," "Green Blues," and "Less Is More"—features a different musical style. Her CD *Grass Roots* contains both lively tunes and slower, sentimental songs such as "A Small Star" and "This River" that seem reminiscent of show tune ballads. Don't miss "Green Christmas" on the *Christmas Heart* CD. All of Earth Mama's works are worthy additions to any environmental collection. 🌳

435 *School House Rock! Earth.*
GRADES: PS–4
DVD. SERIES: SCHOOL HOUSE ROCK. Walt Disney Home Entertainment, 2009, ISBN 978-0-7888-9083-3, $29.95.
SUBJECTS: Environmentalism; Biodiversity conservation; Recycling

The first new School House Rock in 35 years includes ten songs about conservation, pollution, biodiversity, and other environmental topics. Some of the songs like "Solar Power to the People" feature the characteristic School House Rock animation and others like "The Rainforest" has been modernized with more sophisticated animation. Regardless of the animation, School House Rock continues its trend of catchy, educational tunes that are sure to stand the test of time. Children will enjoy the fun tunes and adults will love when nostalgia meets modern sensibilities in this DVD. ♻ 🌳

436 Stoltz, Walkin' Jim. *Come Walk with Me.*
GRADES: PS–2

DVD. Wild Wind Records, 1995, $14. 32 minutes
SUBJECTS: Environmental protection; Songs and music

Featuring seven of Walkin' Jim's favorite songs, this is a musical and visual resource in one. In the 32-minute video, Walkin' Jim and a group of children go on a hike, accompanied by his songs about respecting nature. Alternating between footage of Jim and the children and shots of animals and nature, this video also features brief conversations about the importance of habitat preservation and environmental harmony. Fans of music and fans of nature videos will enjoy this. 🌳

Stoltz, Walkin' Jim.
Wild Wind Records

437 *A Kid for the Wild.*
GRADES: PS–6
CD. 1990, $14.
SUBJECTS: Environmental protection; Songs and music

438 *The Web of Life.*
GRADES: PS–6
CD. 1996, $14.
SUBJECTS: Environmental protection; Songs and music

Walkin' Jim is known for . . . well . . . *walking*. His long nature walks have inspired songs that teach kids about nature and why it is important to respect nature and take care of the earth. A chorus of children often accompanies his deep voice and guitar. *The Web of Life* features songs that explain habitats and how each creature has its place. *A Kid for the Wild* helps children understand the importance of preserving habitats even as they visit and appreciate them. 🌳

Taylor, J. P.
John Paul Taylor, Jr. (BMI)

439 *The Eyes of the World.*
GRADES: PS–6
CD. 2000, $15.
SUBJECTS: Environmental protection—Songs and music; Songs and music

440 *The Last Frontier.*
GRADES: PS–6
CD. 2008, $15.
SUBJECTS: Environmental protection—Songs and music; Songs and music

441 Taylor, J. P., and The Academics. *Singin' for the Earth.*
GRADES: PS–6
CD. 1999, $15.
SUBJECTS: Environmental protection—Songs and music; Songs and music

Each song on these three CDs is devoted to an aspect of environmental concern such as habitat conservation, pollution, and the water cycle. Often folksy, sometimes Caribbean or bluesy, the instrumentals partner with clear and pleasant vocals to deliver simple lyrics that present stories, problems, and encouragement. *Singin' for the Earth* is perhaps better suited for younger kids, with lighter, livelier songs; *The Eyes of the World* is more mellow and sophisticated, and delivers compelling music and environmental concepts that older children and teens will enjoy. *The Last Frontier* has a more soft-rock edge that will appeal to all ages. 🌳

NONFICTION

442 Amsel, Sheri. *365 Ways to Live Green for Kids: Saving the Environment at Home, School, or at Play—Every Day!*
GRADES: 2–4
Adams Media, 2009, pap., ISBN 978-1-60550-634-0, 224p. $7.95.
SUBJECTS: Environmental protection

A simple, useful book for libraries, classrooms, and homes with already well-developed collections. Not all of the tips are hands-on activities (some are simply vocabulary terms) but they all help children to gain a better understanding of conservation. ♻ 🌍

443 Anderson, Tom, and Jeca Taudte. *MySpace/Our Planet: Change Is Possible.*
GRADES: 10–12

Ill. by Dan Santat. HarperCollins, 2008, pap., ISBN 978-0-06-156204-4, 166p. $12.99.
SUBJECTS: Internet and environmentalism

The hugely popular social networking site tries its hand at environmentalism and does a nice job of appealing to its targeted audience. Packed with enough scientific information to make this a legitimate research resource, this book's value lies in quick, easy, and doable environmental tips as well as the extensive resource list. The added feature of tips from MySpace members will no doubt add to this book's popularity. A surprising gem for teen readers, this book is sure to be in demand as long as MySpace remains a favorite. ♻ ✪ ♈

---

444 Andryszewski, Tricia. *Mass Extinction: Examining the Current Crisis.*
GRADES: 6–8
SERIES: DISCOVERY! Twenty-First Century Books, 2007, ISBN 978-0-8225-7523-8, 112p. $31.93.
SUBJECTS: Extinction

Could two-thirds of the earth's species just disappear? This alarming book points to altered habitats, climate change, and poisons (among other things) as possible triggers of a mass extinction. Aimed at older readers, the text is advanced without being too overwhelming, though the subject matter is certainly disturbing. An intriguing resource for teen researchers and a good addition to a well-rounded collection. ✪

---

445 Baines, John. *Food for Life.*
GRADES: 2–4
SERIES: SUSTAINABLE FUTURES. Smart Apple Media, 2007, ISBN 978-1-58340-978-7, 48p. $31.35.
SUBJECTS: Agriculture; Food supply

Is organic food sustainable? What are food miles? What is urban farming? These questions and others are answered in this book in the Sustainable Futures series. Readers will come to understand the food supply and why it is important to focus on food sources that are sustainable and not harmful to the environment. An appealing book on a subject that is a growing concern for environmentalists. ♻ ✪

446 Baird, Nicola. *A Green World?*
GRADES: 3–6
SERIES: VIEWPOINTS. Sea-to-Sea, 2006, ISBN 978-1-932889-57-4,
32p. $27.10.
SUBJECTS: Environmentalism; Environmental protection; Opposing
viewpoints

This book evaluates which is more important: a clean environment or a
growing economy? Is global warming a man-made problem or a natural
change? These questions are addressed by people with different points of
view in this book in the Viewpoints series. The reader is introduced to many
different people and organizations on both sides of the environmental movement. This resource also includes a glossary, organizational contact information, and an index. ✪

447 Ballard, Carol. *The Search for Better Conservation.*
GRADES: 3–6
SERIES: SCIENCE QUEST. Gareth Stevens Publishing, 2005, ISBN 978-
0-8368-4553-2, 32p. $26.00.
SUBJECTS: Nature conservation

An introduction to the ways that science is being used to help conserve natural resources and animal habitats. Four case studies at the end of the book
give examples of real-life conservation efforts to help readers grasp the importance of conservation and the role that science plays in environmental
protection. ✪

448 Barnham, Kay. *Protect Nature.*
GRADES: 1–3
SERIES: ENVIRONMENT ACTION! Crabtree Publishing, 2007, ISBN 978-
0-7787-3658-5, 32p. $26.60.
SUBJECTS: Nature conservation

This book in the Environment Action! series explores environmental conservation. It begins by examining the nature of the issue with large, bright
photographs, definitions, and fast facts. The second half details steps that
children can take to conserve natural resources. The large, simple text, glossaries, and index help beginning readers research conservation issues. ♻ ✪

449 Bellamy, Rufus. *Protecting Habitats.*
GRADES: 4–6
SERIES: ACTION FOR THE ENVIRONMENT. Smart Apple Media, 2006,
ISBN 978-1-58340-600-7, 32p. $27.10.
SUBJECTS: Habitat conservation

Children are often fascinated by animals and their habitats, and this book in
the Action for the Environment series will inspire them to help protect animals and their habitats. Threats to wildlife habitats are clearly presented in
this bright and well-designed book. "Action Stations" in every chapter give
examples of responsible and clever ways to help animals with threatened
habitats. ♻ 🌍

Boothroyd, Jennifer.
SERIES: FIRST STEP NONFICTION—ECOLOGY. Lerner Publishing

450 *Animals and the Environment.*
GRADES: PS–2
2008, ISBN 978-0-8225-8602-9, 23p. $18.60.
SUBJECTS: Animal ecology; Animals; Ecology

451 *People and the Environment.*
GRADES: PS–2
2008, ISBN 978-0-8225-8601-2, 23p. $18.60.
SUBJECTS: Human ecology; Human-plant relationships; Human-
animal relationships

452 *Plants and the Environment.*
GRADES: PS–2
2008, ISBN 978-0-8225-8603-6, 23p. $18.60.
SUBJECTS: Plant ecophysiology; Plant ecology

Designed to ease beginning readers into nonfiction, these books about conservation feature short sentences, large text, vocabulary words, and large
color photographs relating to various conservation activities—usually with
images of young children. 🌍

Calhoun, Yael.
SERIES: ENVIRONMENTAL ISSUES. Chelsea House

453 *Conservation.*
GRADES: 9–12

2005, ISBN 978-0-7910-8203-4, 164p. $31.95.
SUBJECTS: Conservation of natural resources; Nature conservation

454 *Wildlife Protection.*
GRADES: 9–12
2005, ISBN 978-0-7910-8204-1, 164p. $31.95.
SUBJECTS: Wildlife conservation

Each book in this series takes an in-depth look at an environmental issue and how it is related to other environmental concerns—for example, how global warming threatens wildlife. These books use academic language and do not include charts, graphics, or photographs. Each chapter includes articles written by different authors to provide varied perspectives. Bibliographies and extensive indexes add to this series' value as a research resource for high school collections.

---

455 Coley, Mary McIntyre. *Environmentalism: How You Can Make a Difference.*
GRADES: 3–6
SERIES: TAKE ACTION. Capstone Press, 2009, ISBN 978-1-4296-2797-9, 32p. $18.99.
SUBJECTS: Environmental protection

Perfect for readers who really want to get involved, this volume in the Take Action series guides children step-by-step through the process of participation and presents examples of real-life children in "Action Spotlights." It encourages children to identify environmental problems, brainstorm ideas, research solutions, and set an action plan. Includes a list of organizational resources

---

456 Daynes, Katie, and Peter Allen. *See Inside Planet Earth: With Over 80 Flaps to Lift.*
GRADES: 1–3
SERIES: AN EXPLORER'S GUIDE. Usborne Books, 2008, ISBN 978-0-7945-2070-0, 15p. $12.99.
SUBJECTS: Environmental protection; Earth; Toys and movable books

Lift-the-flap features hide facts and tips all over the pages, making this book a fun, hands-on experience for children and parents alike. This interactive guide to Earth and its threats includes greenhouse gases, global warming, melting glaciers, and climate change. Brief, but packed with information.

457   De Rothschild, David, consultant ed. *Earth Matters: An
Encyclopedia of Ecology.*
GRADES: 3–6
DK Children, 2008, ISBN 978-0-7566-3435-3, 256p. $24.99.
SUBJECTS: Ecology; Conservation of natural resources

This book is a must-have resource for elementary schools. Dubbed "an encyclopedia of ecology," it provides just the right amount of information on
ecological matters and the environments found in different biomes. It also
addresses how the reader can make a difference. Large color photographs,
graphics, and footprints with conservation tips are found throughout the
book. A thorough index makes this resource one of the most comprehensive
resources for this age range. ●

Desonie, Dana.
SERIES: OUR FRAGILE PLANET. Chelsea House

458   *Biosphere: Ecosystems and Biodiversity Loss.*
GRADES: 6–12
2007, ISBN 978-0-8160-6219-5, 194p. $35.00.
SUBJECTS: Biosphere; Biodiversity conservation

459   *Geosphere: The Land and Its Uses.*
GRADES: 6–12
2007, ISBN 978-0-8160-6217-1, 194p. $35.00.
SUBJECTS: Land use—Environmental aspects; Nature—Effect of
human beings on

Part of the Our Fragile Planet series, these entries address the impact that humans are having on the biosphere and geosphere. Photographs, charts, and
diagrams combine with bold-type vocabulary words, a glossary, and an index
to give a textbook-like feel to these volumes. The result is a comprehensive
look at each global issue in a format familiar to middle school students. Recommended for the serious environmental researcher. ⬡ ●

460   Driscoll, Michael, and Dennis Driscoll. *A Child's Introduction to the
Environment: The Air, Earth, and Sea Around Us—Plus
Experiments, Projects, and Activities You Can Do to Help Our Planet.*
GRADES: 3–6

Ill. by Meredith Hamilton. Black Dog & Leventhal, 2008, ISBN 978-1-57912-429-8, 96p. $19.95.

SUBJECTS: Environmental science; Environmentalism

A brilliant combination of informative text, colorful illustrations, activities, and anecdotes, this book is a must-have resource for environmental collections. The text is clearly written and efficiently highlights important terms. Activities range from environmental experiments to conservation efforts. The authors have a clear understanding of the language and ideas that appeal to young readers. ♺ ❂ ❦

---

461 Dudley, William, ed. *The Environment.*

GRADES: 10–12

SERIES: THE HISTORY OF ISSUES. Greenhaven Press, 2006, ISBN 978-0-7377-2865-1, 224p. $34.95.

SUBJECTS: Environmentalism; Opposing viewpoints

Part of the Opposing Viewpoints series, the History of Issues series presents historical essays, documents, speeches, and legal cases on controversial matters. *The Environment* includes four broad chapters that begin with the early conservation movement and continue through modern issues. Each article has a distinct perspective, allowing students to see all sides of the topic. The bibliography, timeline, and detailed index aid researchers. ❂

---

462 Dupler, Douglas, ed. *Conserving the Environment.*

GRADES: 9–12

SERIES: OPPOSING VIEWPOINTS. Greenhaven Press, 2006, ISBN 978-0-7377-3313-6, 243p. $37.40.

SUBJECTS: Environmental protection; Environmental degradation; Energy conservation; Opposing viewpoints

Examining many environmental hot topics such as global warming, energy resources, deforestation, and overpopulation, *Conserving the Environment* provides students with a multileveled understanding of the issues. The annotated bibliography and comprehension questions provide further fodder for research. If budgets allow for only one environmental book in the Opposing Viewpoints series, this book does an admirable job of representing a wide range of environmental concerns. ❂

463 Farquhar, Jackie. *Try This at Home: Planet-Friendly Projects for Kids.*
GRADES: 3–6
Owlkids Books, 2008, pap., ISBN 978-2-895791-92-8, 94p. $10.95.
SUBJECTS: Environmental education

How will you score on the eco-IQ quiz? This entertaining, activity-packed book encourages children and teens to become more active in the environment. It includes twenty eco-friendly projects and statistical information stressing the importance of conservation. Projects are clear, well explained, and accompanied by photographs and illustrations. A fun addition to your collection with definite tween appeal, this a wise choice for this age group.

464 Garrett, Leslie. *Earth Smart: How to Take Care of the Environment.*
GRADES: PS–2
DK Publishing, 2006, ISBN 978-0-7566-1912-1, 32p. $14.99.
SUBJECTS: Environmental protection

Sophie and Spencer spend an enlightening day with their aunt Charlotte, an environmental studies teacher, in this beginning reader. The text and photographs help teach Sophie, Spencer, and the reader the importance of taking care of the environment. Facts and tips are woven into the conversation between Aunt Charlotte and the children, making this book a pleasant read.

465 Gilpin, Daniel. *Transportation Solutions.*
GRADES: 4–6
SERIES: ACTION FOR THE ENVIRONMENT. Smart Apple Media, 2006, ISBN 978-1-58340-599-4, 32p. $27.10.
SUBJECTS: Transportation—Environmental aspects

Problems created by transportation—and new solutions to those problems—are presented using large, easy-to-read text and bold, relevant photographs. Each chapter features "Action Stations" that show young readers how to use transportation wisely.

466 Guillain, Charlotte. *Caring for Nature.*
GRADES: PS–2
SERIES: HELP THE ENVIRONMENT. Heinemann, 2008, ISBN 978-1-4329-0889-8, 24p. $20.71.
SUBJECTS: Nature conservation

By using simple words and repetitive phrases, this book helps children recognize ecological terms, become more environmentally conscious, and learn to read. The text is large and easy to read and is accompanied by large descriptive photographs of children caring for nature. The simple picture glossary and index introduce young readers to research tools and the broad subject of nature conservation. ♻ 🌳

467 Hewitt, Sally. *Your Local Environment.*
GRADES: 2–5
SERIES: GREEN TEAM. Crabtree Publishing, 2009, ISBN 978-0-7787-4100-8, 32p. $26.60.
SUBJECTS: Environmental protection

Children will learn to think globally and act locally in this title in the new Green Team series. Environmental activities, graphics, and photographs emphasize the importance of respect for the environment. Up-to-date statistics and other information are delivered in age-appropriate language to ensure comprehension. ♻ 🌐

468 Hirschmann, Kris. *Going Green.*
GRADES: 3–5
SERIES: RIPPED FROM THE HEADLINES: THE ENVIRONMENT. Erickson, 2008, ISBN 978-1-60217-025-4, 64p. $23.95.
SUBJECTS: Environmental protection; Conservation of natural resources

What does it mean to "go green"? Charts, vocabulary words, photographs, and facts explain that this trend is more than just a fad. Quotations on the subject from a wide range of sources are well documented in the back of the book, along with a bibliography and an index. This book does a good job of presenting a balanced (if not brief) look at what is involved in "going green." 🌐

PROJECTS AND BOOKS THAT SUPPORT THEM

1. Plant a tree (or trees) to balance the paper used in your home, library, or classroom. For younger children: *Wangari's Trees of Peace* by Jeanette Winter, *Paul Bunyan's Sweetheart* by Marybeth Lorbiecki, and *The Lorax* by Dr. Seuss. For older children: *Riding the Flume* by Patricia Curtis Pfitsch and *Hoot* by Carl Hiaasen.

2. Adopt a playground or road and work together to keep it clean. For younger children: *Trash Trouble* by Larry Dane Brimner, *Abigale the Happy Whale* by Peter Farrelly. For older children: *Earth's Garbage Crisis* by Christine Dorion and *The Everything Kids' Environment Book: Learn How You Can Help Save the Environment—By Getting Involved at School, at Home and at Play* by Sheri Amsel.

3. Create a flower or vegetable garden to educate and raise awareness in your community. For younger children: *The Apple-Pip Princess* by Jane Ray, *On Meadowview Street* by Henry Cole. For older children: *Conserving the Environment* by John Woodward and Jennifer Skancke and *Biodiversity* by Debra A. Miller.

4. Start a recycling program in your community (if there is already a recycling program, have a recycled art or fashion show to raise awareness of the program). For younger children: *Why Should I Recycle?* by Jen Green, *Michael Recycle* by Ellie Bethel and *The Adventures of a Plastic Bottle* by Alison Inches. For older children: *Judy Moody Saves the World* by Megan McDonald, *MySpace/Our Planet: Change Is Possible* by Tom Anderson and Jeca Taudte, and *Generation Green: The Ultimate Teen Guide to Living an Eco-Friendly Life* by Linda and Tosh Sivertsen.

5. Ride your bike or carpool to the store, school, or work to limit air pollution and greenhouse gases. (Promote May as National Bike Month and encourage friends, family, and the entire school to ride their bikes!) For younger children: *Winston of Churchill: One Bear's Battle Against Global Warming* by Jean Davies Okimoto, *Snowy White World to Save* by Stephanie Lisa Tara, and *The Polar Bears' Home* by Laura Bergen. For older children: *Bodies in the Ice: Melting Glaciers and the Recovery of the Past* by James M. Dean, *How We Know What We Know About Our Changing Climate: Scientists and Kids Explore Global Warming* and *A Hot Planet Needs Cool Kids: Understanding Climate Change and What You Can Do About It* by Julie Hall.

469 Jackson, Kay. *Rainforests.*

GRADES: 3–6

SERIES: OUR ENVIRONMENT. Kidhaven Press, 2007, ISBN 978-0-7377-3624-3, 48p. $26.20.

SUBJECTS: Rain forest ecology; Rain forests

A lively discussion of why rain forests are important, what is threatening them, and what can be done to protect them. Readers will gain a broad understanding of the subject matter and may continue their research using the multimedia bibliography in the back of this book. Part of the Our Environment series. ◉

470 Jakab, Cheryl. *Biodiversity.*

GRADES: 3–6

SERIES: GLOBAL ISSUES. Smart Apple Media, 2008, ISBN 978-1-59920-124-5, 32p. $27.10.

SUBJECTS: Biodiversity

The idea of biodiversity can be a difficult concept for younger readers. However, this book offers case studies to help explain the importance of ensuring environmental diversification. Information about global threats to biodiversity and their solutions gives the reader a more robust understanding of the issue. Appealing design, bright illustrations, and clear language make the information accessible to readers. ◉

471 Jankeliowitch, Anne. *50 Ways to Save the Earth.*

GRADES: 4–6

Abrams Books, 2008, ISBN 978-0-8109-7239-1, 144p. $17.95.

SUBJECTS: Environmental protection; Conservation of natural resources

Exactly what the title says, this book details fifty different ways we can help save the earth. Each tip is reinforced with large color photographs, scientific information explaining why the tip is important and a tangible idea to reinforce the tip. Sprinkled throughout the book are anecdotal stories of animals and communities that are affected by such dangers as pollution and global warming. This book is both beautiful and useful and while suitable for students as young as fourth grade, could appeal to readers of much higher reading levels. ♻ ◉ 🏆

....

472 Kidd, J. S., and Renee A. Kidd. *Agricultural Versus Environmental Science.*

GRADES: 9–12

SERIES: SCIENCE AND SOCIETY. Chelsea House, 2006, ISBN 978-0-8160-5608-8, 176p. $35.00.

SUBJECTS: Environmental science; Agricultural science; Green Revolution

Aimed at high school students, this title lacks color (the photographs are black-and-white) but the meaty text packs a punch. It discusses key figures on each side of this "battle," significant historical facts, legislation, and hot-button issues. Serious researchers and environmental science students will find this resource interesting and timely. Part of the Science and Society series. 🌐

....

473 Knight, M. J. *Why Should I Care About Nature?*

GRADES: 2–4

SERIES: ONE SMALL STEP. Smart Apple Media, 2009, ISBN 978-1-59920-266-2, 32p. $27.10.

SUBJECTS: Nature conservation

Readers will learn about the importance of stewardship in this book in the One Small Step series. Each two-page spread includes "I Can Make a Difference" boxes with environmental tips and "One Small Fact" bubbles about nature and its value. This book also includes a glossary, Web sites, and an index and is a useful resource for impressing upon a young reader the importance of caring for our environment. ♻ 🌐

....

474 Koellhoffer, Tara, ed. *The Environment.*

GRADES: 4–6

SERIES: SCIENCE NEWS FOR KIDS. Chelsea Clubhouse, 2006, ISBN 978-0-7910-9123-4, 122p. $30.00.

SUBJECTS: Environmental protection; Pollution; Nature conservation

Science News for Kids is a magazine that has been in publication since 1922 and has adapted its articles to reflect changing demands for information. This book is a compilation of articles on environmental issues from various authors. Each article is accompanied by comprehension questions before and after the article as well as in separate text boxes throughout the article. The book's value lies in the text, questions, and bibliographic and online resources; it contains no graphics or illustrations. ☻

....

475 Lim, Cheng Puay. *Vanishing Forests.*
GRADES: 2–4
SERIES: GREEN ALERT! Raintree Publishers, 2004, ISBN 978-0-7398-7012-9, 48p. $31.43.
SUBJECTS: Deforestation; Nature—Effect of human beings on

An eye-catching design helps to keep readers interested in this book about the reasons for and solutions to deforestation. By using tools including case studies, environmental tips, a glossary, an index, and a bibliography, this book provides a rich introduction to the subject of deforestation. ♳ ☻

....

476 *Living Green.*
GRADES: 6–9
SERIES: LIVING GREEN. World Book, 2009, ISBN 978-0-7166-1400-5, $279.00.
SUBJECTS: Sustainability; Pollution; Conservation

This set of nine volumes includes titles that address the issues of pollution, sustainable goods, green architecture, and transportation. Each book in the set uses fact boxes to present current statistical information, vocabulary terms relating to the subject, and activities and summary boxes that help students better understand the content. This environmental set presents a comprehensive look at sustainability. Students will appreciate the easy-to-understand layout and parents and teachers will appreciate another trusted resource from World Book. ♳ ☻

....

477 Lorbiecki, Marybeth. *Planet Patrol: A Kids' Action Guide to Earth Care.*
GRADES: 3–5
Ill. by Nancy Meyers. Two-Can Publishing, 2005, ISBN 978-1-58728-514-1, 48p. $15.95.
SUBJECTS: Ecology; Environmental science

This lively and creative book gives young readers the tools they need to actively care for the earth. Information about environmental issues such as habitat conservation, pollution, energy conservation, and recycling is followed by action tips for new planet patrol members. The design is very inviting to young readers. Also included is an extensive bibliography, a glossary, and an index. ⊕ ● ♔

---

478 McKay, Kim, and Jenny Bonnin. *True Green Kids: 100 Things You Can Do to Save the Planet.*
GRADES: 3–6
National Geographic, 2008, pap., ISBN 978-1-4263-0442-2, 144p. $15.95.
SUBJECTS: Environmental responsibility; Conservation of natural resources

Packed with 100 easy and fun environmental activities for home, outdoors, at school, at the store, and even on vacation, this children's version of *True Green* puts the responsibility for conservation in young people's hands. Children will be empowered through creativity to become environmental heroes in their communities. ⊕ ● ♔

---

479 McLeish, Ewan. *Rain Forest Destruction.*
GRADES: 5–7
SERIES: WHAT IF WE DO NOTHING? World Almanac Library, 2007, ISBN 978-0-8368-7758-8, 48p. $31.00.
SUBJECTS: Rain forest ecology; Rain forest conservation

What will the earth look like if nothing is done to prevent the destruction of the rain forests? This book explores why these forests are threatened and the steps that can be taken to prevent this crisis from escalating. Plainly written text, fast facts, charts, tables, photographs, a glossary, and an index are all features of this book. Readers are encouraged to consider solutions to this environmental problem. ⊕ ●

---

480 Miller, Debra A., ed. *Biodiversity.*
GRADES: 7–12
SERIES: CURRENT CONTROVERSIES. Greenhaven Press, 2008, ISBN 978-0-7377-3952-7, 196p. $37.40.
SUBJECTS: Biodiversity

The Current Controversies series uses brief, age-appropriate, and varied articles to provide comprehensive examinations of controversial subjects. In this book in the series, articles address biodiversity issues including causes of extinction, food production's impact on biodiversity, and biotechnology. A list of organizations to contact, a bibliography, and an index are also included. ☻

....

481 Morris, Neil. *Looking After My Environment.*
GRADES: K–3
SERIES: GREEN KIDS. QEB, 2008, ISBN 978-1-5956-6543-0, 24p. $24.25.
SUBJECTS: Environmental protection

Playful layouts and a generous amount of photographs add life to this book in the Green Kids series. Peppered throughout the text are relevant statistics about conservation that are easy for this age range to understand (for example, "5 energy-saving light bulbs use the same amount of electricity as 1 ordinary light bulb"). Quirky illustrations feature kid-friendly characters and arrows pointing out important information and there are "You Can Do It!" boxes. Includes an index. ♻ ☻ ♣

....

482 Nakaya, Andrea C. *The Environment.*
GRADES: 7–12
SERIES: ISSUES ON TRIAL. Greenhaven Press, 2006, ISBN 978-0-7377-2797-5, 128p. $34.95.
SUBJECTS: Environmental policy; Environmental ethics

This book in the Issues on Trial series covers four legal cases that have affected the environmental movement. After examining each case, experts offer reactions to it. The last part of the book includes a list of organizations and a bibliography for further research. This book fills a void in serious environmental collections. ☻

....

483 Olien, Rebecca. *Kids Care! 75 Ways to Make a Difference for People, Animals, and the Environment.*
GRADES: 2–4
Ill. by Michael Kline. Williamson Books, 2007, pap., ISBN 978-0-8249-6793-2, 128p. $12.99.
SUBJECTS: Citizenship; Activism; Recycling

While only two chapters are devoted to wildlife and the environment, this entire book invites young people to become active in their communities. The ideas are creative and easy, and the cartoon illustrations are lively. Even the nonenvironmental activities are Earth-friendly and use biodegradable and recyclable materials. ♲ ☻ ♠

---

484 Parker, Russ. *Wildlife Crisis.*
GRADES: 3–6
SERIES: PLANET IN CRISIS. Rosen Publishing, 2009, ISBN 978-1-4358-5255-6, 32p. $25.25.
SUBJECTS: Wildlife conservation; Endangered species

Contemporary layouts that are busy and bright invite readers to explore the impact of deforestation, overpopulation, and the destruction of habitats. Like the other books in the Planet in Crisis series, this book is large in size and features two-page spreads, "hot topic" boxes, progression charts, and diagrams. It also includes organizational contacts, a bibliography, an index, and a glossary. ♲ ☻

---

485 Parks, Peggy J. *Ecotourism.*
GRADES: 3–6
SERIES: OUR ENVIRONMENT. Kidhaven Press, 2005, ISBN 978-0-7377-3048-7, 48p. $26.20.
SUBJECTS: Ecotourism

Can tourism hurt the environment? Or can it be used to raise awareness and promote positive changes? This book presents students with another facet to environmentalism that they may not have considered. ☻

---

486 Petersen, Christine. *Conservation.*
GRADES: PS–2
SERIES: A TRUE BOOK. Scholastic, 2004, ISBN 978-0-516-22805-1, 47p. $25.00.
SUBJECTS: Conservation of natural resources

Petersen helps young readers understand conservation in this entry in the True Book series. The short chapters discuss the conservation of Earth's natural resources, species, and wilderness. The "Important Words" section and an index add to this book's usefulness. ♲ ☻

487 Pipe, Jim. *Ecosystems.*
GRADES: 1–3
SERIES: EARTHWISE. Stargazer Books, 2005, ISBN 978-1-932799-50-7, 32p. $27.10.
SUBJECTS: Ecosystems; Nature conservation

A careful, well-designed introduction to the concept of ecosystems. The short paragraphs help younger readers move through the information. Conservation facts are paired with helpful and doable tips for readers to put what they learn into action. ♲ ♼

488 Rapp, Valerie. *Protecting Earth's Land.*
GRADES: 3–5
SERIES: SAVING OUR LIVING EARTH. Lerner Publishing, 2009, ISBN 978-0-8225-7559-7, 71p. $30.60.
SUBJECTS: Environmental science; Environmentalism; Green movement

Readers will learn about historical events, including legislation, that have affected how land is protected and conserved. Real children and young adults working to improve the environment are featured throughout the book in bright photographs. The detailed text, rich layout, bibliography, index, and glossary are nice features that are included in all the books in this series. ♲ ♼

Royston, Angela.
SERIES: PROTECT OUR PLANET. Heinemann

489 *Disappearing Forests.*
GRADES: K–2
2008, ISBN 978-1-4329-0927-7, 32p. $25.36.
SUBJECTS: Deforestation; Forest conservation

490 *Disappearing Wildlife.*
GRADES: K–2
2008, ISBN 978-1-4329-0928-4, 32p. $25.36.
SUBJECTS: Endangered species; Wildlife conservation

The first half of each book is devoted to exploring the environmental concerns of deforestation and threatened wildlife habitats using large text, vocabulary words, charts, maps, and descriptive photographs. The second half uses the same tactics to feature how humans are beginning to protect these natural resources—globally and locally. Each book includes a glossary, an index, and a multimedia bibliography. ⊛ ☻

....

491   Sachidhanandam, Uma. *Threatened Habitats.*
GRADES: 2–4
SERIES: GREEN ALERT! Raintree Publishers, 2004, ISBN 978-1-84421-667-3, 48p.
SUBJECTS: Nature conservation; Nature—Effect of human beings on

How are habitats threatened? What is being done about these threats? Case studies integrated into this book help illustrate the importance of protecting habitats, and practical tips give readers ideas to aid in the effort to save threatened habitats. This book also includes a glossary, an index, and a bibliography. ⊛ ☻

....

492   Smith, Natalie. *Habitat Protection.*
GRADES: 2–4
SERIES: SAVING OUR WORLD. Marshall Cavendish, 2008, ISBN 978-0-7614-3225-8, 32p. $28.50.
SUBJECTS: Habitat conservation; Environmentalism

Large, dramatic photographs, comprehension questions, and plenty of environmental tips engage the reader while also delivering information about the importance of protecting natural habitats for both humans and wildlife. This book does an admirable job of keeping the material interesting and providing high-quality information about the subject. ⊛ ☻

....

493   Spilsbury, Louise. *Food and Agriculture: How We Use the Land.*
GRADES: 3–6
SERIES: GEOGRAPHY FOCUS. Raintree Publishers, 2006, ISBN 978-1-4109-1114-8, 48p. $31.43.
SUBJECTS: Agriculture; Food supply

Agricultural use of the land affects the environment in many different ways with varying ecological consequences. Photographs, diagrams, and charts keep the reader's attention while conveying this complicated concept succinctly. Vocabulary words, a glossary, a bibliography, and an index add to the value of this book. Attractive, dynamic, and contemporary, this is part of the Geography Focus series. ❸

....

494 Spilsbury, Richard. *The Great Outdoors: Saving Habitats.*
GRADES: 3–5
SERIES: YOU CAN SAVE THE PLANET. Heinemann, 2005, ISBN 978-1-4034-6847-5, 32p. $19.75.
SUBJECTS: Habitat conservation

What are habitats and ecosystems? How have people changed them? Through bright, dramatic pictures and many hands-on Taking Action features, this book shows that children can help to conserve our environment's habitats. Case Study sections feature inspiring stories of real children who have improved habitats near them.

....

495 Stewart, Melissa. *A Place for Butterflies.*
GRADES: 2–4
Ill. by Higgins Bond. Peachtree Publishers, 2006, ISBN 978-1-56145-357-3, 32p. $16.95.
SUBJECTS: Butterflies—Effect of human beings on

Colorful pages featuring butterfly habitats and easy-to-read text express the need for humans to make a place for butterflies for ecological balance. Each page also displays fact boxes with more detailed information about butterflies for the more advanced reader. ♻ ❸

....

496 Stille, Darlene R. *Nature Interrupted: The Science of Environmental Chain Reactions.*
GRADES: 5–7
SERIES: HEADLINE SCIENCE. Compass Point Books, 2009, ISBN 978-0-7565-3949-8, 48p. $20.99.
SUBJECTS: Environmental chemistry

Each chapter in this book about the delicate natural balance begins with a recent quote from a recognizable news source such as CBS and the *New York Times*. The book uses contemporary layouts, dramatic photographs, historical fact boxes, and a timeline to relay information about the chain reactions that occur when one element of a habitat is altered by pollution, deforestation, or even the use of pesticides. Includes bibliographic resources, a glossary, and source notes. ✪

....

497 Welsbacher, Anne. *Protecting Earth's Rain Forests.*
GRADES: 3–5
SERIES: SAVING OUR LIVING EARTH. Lerner Publishing, 2009, ISBN 978-0-8225-7562-7, 71p. $30.60.
SUBJECTS: Rain forest ecology

Readers will learn that although rain forests are threatened, progress has been made toward preventing further damage. Examples of real children and young adults working to protect the rain forest—and boxes with interesting facts about rain forests—add to the appeal. Another excellent book in the Saving Our Earth series, this book includes detailed scientific facts, a vibrant layout, an index, a bibliography, and a glossary. ♻ ✪

....

498 West, Krista, ed. *Critical Perspectives on Environmental Protection.*
GRADES: 9–12
SERIES: SCIENTIFIC AMERICAN CRITICAL ANTHOLOGIES ON ENVIRONMENT AND CLIMATE. Rosen Publishing, 2006, ISBN 978-1-4042-0691-5, 224p. $31.95.
SUBJECTS: Environmental protection

The books in this series consist of collections of *Scientific American* articles originally published between 1995 and 2005 that relate to environmental protection. Most of the articles include black-and-white graphics such as diagrams, charts, and illustrations to complement the text. High school students will find these useful for reports about politics, the environment, and activism. ✪

....

499 Wheeler, Jill C. *Everyday Conservation.*
GRADES: 2–4
SERIES: EYE ON ENERGY. Abdo Publishing, 2007, ISBN 978-1-59928-804-8, 32p. $24.21.
SUBJECTS: Energy conservation

This powerful new series employs dynamic design, colorful photographs featuring children and many useful conservation tips. Without sacrificing factual information, the layout engages readers with "Fact or Fiction" boxes and "Energy Buzz" boxes. The relevance of the information, combined with the style of the layout, makes this book a very smart purchase for the children's nonfiction collection. ♺ ✹

500 Woodward, John, and Jennifer Skancke, eds. *Conserving the Environment.*
GRADES: 7–12
SERIES: CURRENT CONTROVERSIES. Greenhaven Press, 2006, ISBN 978-0-7377-2476-9, 248p. $34.95.
SUBJECTS: Environmental protection

The Current Controversies series uses brief, age-appropriate, and varied articles to thoroughly examine controversial subjects. Included articles address such issues as humans' effect on global warming, the value of sustainable farming, and the importance of biodiversity. Each title in this series includes a list of organizations to contact, a bibliography, and an index. ✹

RECYCLED FAVORITES

Fiction

501 Bang, Molly. *Common Ground: The Water, Earth, and Air We Share.*
GRADES: K–4
Ill. by the author. Blue Sky Press, 1997, ISBN 978-0-590-10056-4, 32p. $14.95.
SUBJECTS: Environmentalism—Fiction; Environmental protection—Fiction

Inspired by Garrett Hardin's 1968 essay "The Tragedy of the Commons," this picture book tells the story of a common area that is rich with natural resources. Because the common ground belongs to everyone, everyone uses it and it falls victim to the consequences of overpopulation. Bang punctuates the legend and reality of her story with vibrant illustrations that tell a story within a story. Pay special attention to the illustrations, as they portray how human behavior is affected by overpopulation and depletion of resources. This book can help start a dialogue with children about how resources should be respected; it also promotes sustainable living. 🌳

502   Cherry, Lynne. *The Dragon and the Unicorn.*
GRADES: 1–3
Ill. by the author. Gulliver Green, 1995, ISBN 978-0-15-224193-3, 40p. $16.00.
SUBJECTS: Conservation of natural resources—Fiction

Valerio, a dragon, and Allegra, a unicorn, live peacefully in the Ardet Forest until humans enter the picture and the human king begins to cut down the trees. The animals must work with a child princess to save the forest. Beautiful, detailed illustrations whimsically depict this environmental fairy tale, a timeless story that can help children understand deforestation and the need for conservation. 🌳

503   Cherry, Lynne. *The Great Kapok Tree: A Tale of the Amazon Rain Forest.*
GRADES: PS–2
Ill. by the author. Gulliver Green, 1990, ISBN 978-0-15-200520-7, 40p. $17.00.
SUBJECTS: Conservation of natural resources—Fiction; Rain forests—Fiction; Ecology—Fiction

A man intending to chop down the majestic kapok tree in the Amazon rain forest lies down to take a nap and is visited by animals who explain why the rain forest is important to them. Cherry's colorful illustrations take up most of the two-page spreads and provide an up-close, detailed look at the animals in their vibrant habitat. An excellent book to share one-on-one or as a read-aloud. 🌳

504   de Yonge, Sandra Chisholm. *The Last Bit Bear: A Fable.*
GRADES: PS–2
Ill. by Ellen Meloy. Roberts Rinehart, 2004, pap., ISBN 978-1-57098-431-0, 46p. $7.95.
SUBJECTS: Pollution—Fiction; Conservation of natural resources—Fiction; Bears—Fiction; Natural parks and reserves—Fiction

First published in 1984, this book is still as valuable as when it was first released. Clover, a bit-bear, depends on a sole food source that has disappeared because of the "other animal." Clover embarks on a journey to find the moak trees he needs to survive and meets other animals along the way who have also been affected by the "other animal." This tale, sweetly illustrated with pen-and-ink and watercolor illustrations, shows how human actions affect entire ecosystems. ♣

505 Gerson, Mary-Joan. *Why the Sky Is Far Away: A Nigerian Folktale.*
GRADES: K–2
Ill. by Carla Golembe. Little, Brown, 1994, ISBN 978-0-316-30852-6, unpaged. $16.45.
SUBJECTS: Folklore; Conservation of natural resources—Fiction

In this Nigerian folktale, the sky used to be so close to the Earth that people could reach up and break off pieces to eat. This was how they received nourishment. But the people began to misuse the sky, wasting the resource it provided. So the sky moved out of reach and the people were forced to learn how to sow and harvest crops. This cautionary tale is complemented by the characteristically African illustrations that are both colorful and expressive. An excellent read-aloud for young audiences. ♣

506 Tresselt, Alvin. *The Gift of the Tree.*
GRADES: 1–3
Ill. by Henri Sorensen. Lothrop, Lee, and Shepard, 1992, ISBN 978-0-688-10684-3, 32p. $14.00.
SUBJECTS: Forest ecology—Fiction

This beautifully illustrated story helps children understand the importance of conservation—and of letting nature take its course. The main character is an oak tree that serves as a food source, living habitat, and shelter. The illustrations bring the role of the tree to life, showing the oak in its various stages of existence and the forest animals that depend on it for their survival. This is a timeless tale perfect for starting a conversation with children about conservation, habitat protection, and decomposition. ♣

Nonfiction

507 Suzuki, David, and Kathy Vanderlinden. *Eco-Fun: Great Projects, Experiments, and Games for a Greener Earth.*
GRADES: 3–6
Greystone Books, 2001, pap., ISBN 978-1-55054-823-5, 128p. $14.95.
SUBJECTS: Environmental education; Environmental science; Science projects

This book by one of the most respected voices in the environmental movement is a must-have for science teachers and environmental educators because it provides forty-eight environmental science activities perfect for pairing with lesson plans. Includes "What's Going On" boxes to explain the science behind the activities. The projects in this book will remain relevant for many years to come. ♺ ◐ ♣

CONSERVATION STORYTIME

Begin with "Good Morning, Dear Earth."

> *Good morning, dear Earth*
> *Good morning, dear Sun (hold your hands above your head)*
> *Good morning, dear stones (put a "stone" in your hand)*
> *And the flowers, every one. (make your hand into a flower)*
>
> *Good morning, dear bees (fly a "bee" around between your fingers)*
> *And the birds in the trees (make your arms into wings and flap them)*
> *Good morning to you (point to the children)*
> *And good morning to me. (point to yourself)*

> *"Good morning, children. Today we are going to talk and read books about taking care of the Earth. What is the Earth? The Earth is the dirt and grass, rivers and oceans, trees, plants, and flowers. The Earth is also you and me. All of us are part of the Earth, and just like your mommy and daddy take care of you, we need to take care of the Earth so it doesn't get hurt. One way that we can take care of the Earth is by keeping it clean."*

Read *The Trouble with Dragons* by Debi Gliori (see entry 408).

Sprinkle paper scraps around the room and, as you sing, walk around with a trash bin for the children to put scraps in.

Sing "We Don't Pollute" (to the tune of "Ten Little Indians").

> *Picking up trash, and putting it in the garbage*
> *Picking up trash, and putting it in the garbage*
> *Picking up trash, and putting it in the garbage*
> *Because we don't pollute!*

"Another way that we can help take care of the Earth is to plant trees."

Read *Paul Bunyan's Sweetheart* by Marybeth Lorbiecki (see entry 416) or *Wangari's Trees of Peace* by Jeanette Winter (see entry 387).

"Can you be a tree? Let's start off as a small acorn before we grow."

Squat down and curl up into a ball and encourage the children to do so.

Sing "Little Acorn" (to the tune of "Pop Goes the Weasel").

> *Little acorn in the ground*
> *Sitting oh-so-still.*
> *Little acorn will you sprout?*
> *Yay! Yes I will! (On "Yay!" Jump up and stretch out your arms)*
>
> *(repeat a couple of times)*

"There are places all over the Earth that are just as wonderful as our city and country. Those places need protecting too. One of those places is the Arctic, where the polar bears live; the ice that they live on is melting. Let's read a story about that."

Read *Snowy White World to Save* by Stephanie Lisa Tara (see entry 7).

"There are things that we can do to keep the ice from melting. Stand up and sing this song with me."

Sing "Help Save the Earth" (to the tune of "Here We Go 'Round the Mulberry Bush").

> *This is the way we walk to the store (walk in place)*
> *Walk to the store, walk to the store*
> *This is the way we walk to the store*
> *To help save the Earth.*

Second verse: This is the way we turn off the lights (put your arms in the air and bring them down to cover your eyes)
Third verse: This is the way we take the bus (sit down and stand up)

"Thank you for coming to storytime today, I hope you remember to love our Earth by keeping it clean, planting trees, and conserving energy."

Sing "If You Love Earth and You Know It" (to the tune of "If You're Happy and You Know It").

If you love Earth and you know it, clap your hands!
If you love Earth and you know it, clap your hands!
If you love Earth and you know it, then let your actions show it!
If you love Earth and you know it, clap your hands!

Second verse: If you love Earth and you know it, stomp your feet!

Third verse: If you love Earth and you know it, shout "Reduce!"
If you love Earth and you know it, shout "Reuse!"
If you love Earth and you know it, then let your actions show it!
If you love Earth and you know it, shout "Recycle!"

APPENDIX 1:

ACCESS BY SYMBOL

References are to entry numbers, not page numbers.

Tree Symbol ♣

Indicates that the title has a lively or heart-filled tone. When this symbol is used alone, it generally means that the book is more entertaining than educational. When looking for books to read aloud or to use for a storytime, look for this symbol.

Tree Symbol 🌳 *(cont.)*

Earth Symbol ◑

Indicates that the title contains a generous amount of factual information. Look for this symbol to help a child or teen with an assignment or research question.

Earth Symbol 🌐 *(cont.)*

Recycle Symbol ♻

Indicates that the title contains practical and useful environmental tips for children and teens. Use this symbol to help children who are interested in getting involved in conservation efforts.

Triple Solutions ♻ 🌐 🏆

These titles that have all three symbols are fun, educational, and environmentally useful.

APPENDIX 2:

ACCESS BY SERIES

AUTHOR INDEX

References are to entry numbers, not page numbers.

TITLE INDEX

References are to entry numbers, not page numbers.

SUBJECT/ GRADE LEVEL INDEX

References are to entry numbers, not page numbers.

Recycling—Fiction

Refuse and refuse disposal

ABOUT THE AUTHOR

LINDSEY PATRICK WESSON is the Continuing Education Coordinator for the Tennessee State Library and Archives. She earned her MLIS from the University of Southern Mississippi and her BA in Theatre from Rhodes College in Memphis. As a children's librarian, she worked at the St. Louis Public Library, theMemphis Public Library, and the Sacramento Public Library. She lives in Nashville with her husband, Peter, and English Bulldog, Lucy Lee. One of Lindsey's favorite eco-friendly activities is sewing cloth shopping bags made from recycled fabric for the "Green Bag Lady" (www.greenbaglady.blogspot.com).